Beginning Medical Spanish

Beginning Medical Spanish. Oral Proficiency and Cultural Humility is designed for medical professionals and supporting staff with no prior knowledge of Spanish who need to develop oral language skills and cross-cultural sensitivity to establish relationship-building communication with their Spanish-speaking patients.

This hospital-tested program teaches how to connect with patients of limited English-speaking ability and offer them the quality care they seek. Role-play activities allow students to develop their oral proficiency in meaningful contexts and contribute to a creative and dynamic classroom environment. Written exercises provide opportunity for practice outside the classroom, and audio recordings are available online for use in class and at home. The cultural readings and extensive bibliographical references in each chapter provide students with information about Hispanic values, beliefs and health practices, while teaching them to consider how these may vary with the identity of each individual and the degree of acculturation to US "mainstream" culture.

Whether you are a student preparing to work in a medical environment, or a professional already working with Spanish-speaking patients, the innovative method of hands-on learning though role-playing practice provided in this program will give you the specific skills you need to communicate confidently and respectfully in Spanish.

Parizad T. Dejbord Sawan is Associate Professor of Spanish at The University of Akron, USA. Originally from Palma de Mallorca-Spain, she received an MA degree in French literature from the University of Akron and holds a PhD in Latin American Literature from the University of Michigan. In 2004, she obtained her National Certification from the American Council for the Teaching of Foreign Languages (ACTFL) to be an Official Tester of the Spanish Oral Proficiency Interview (OPI). She initiated a collaboration between Akron Children's Hospital and the University of Akron through the design and implementation of a 3-semester Beginning Medical Spanish program for medical professionals and supporting staff in 2013 and continues to teach all of the classes at the hospital. She is also a member of the national Medical Spanish Taskforce and is currently participating in the project *Engaging Language Professionals for Patient-Centered Outcomes Research in Latinx Communities* with Ohio State University. This project has been funded by a grant from the Patient-Centered Research Outcome Institute.

Beginning Medical Spanish

Oral Proficiency and Cultural Humility

Parizad T. Dejbord Sawan
Spanish List Advisor: Javier Muñoz-Basols

Routledge
Taylor & Francis Group

LONDON AND NEW YORK

First published 2020
by Routledge
2 Park Square, Milton Park, Abingdon, Oxon OX14 4RN

and by Routledge
52 Vanderbilt Avenue, New York, NY 10017

Routledge is an imprint of the Taylor & Francis Group, an informa business

British Library Cataloguing-in-Publication Data
A catalogue record for this book is available from the British Library

Library of Congress Cataloging-in-Publication Data
Names: Dejbord, Parizad Tamara, author.
Title: Beginning medical Spanish: oral proficiency and cultural humility / Parizad T. Dejbord Sawan.
Description: 1. | New York: Routledge, 2020. | Includes bibliographical references and index.
Identifiers: LCCN 2019035235 (print) | LCCN 2019035236 (ebook) Subjects: LCSH: Spanish language—Conversation and phrase books (for medical personnel) | Spanish language—Textbooks for foreign speakers—English.
Classification: LCC PC4120.M3 D47 2020 (print) | LCC PC4120.M3 (ebook) | DDC 468.3/42102461—dc23
LC record available at https://lccn.loc.gov/2019035235
LC ebook record available at https://lccn.loc.gov/2019035236

ISBN: 978-0-367-32240-3 (hbk)
ISBN: 978-0-367-32243-4 (pbk)
ISBN: 978-0-429-31747-7 (ebk)

Typeset in Times New Roman
by codeMantra

Visit the eResources: www.routledge.com/9780367322434

Para mi Niko, con todo el amor del mundo.

Contents

Acknowledgments

In the Spring of 2013, I initiated a collaboration between Akron Children's Hospital and the Spanish section of the Department of Modern Languages at the University of Akron through the design and implementation of a 3-semester, 9-credit *Certificate of Beginning Medical Spanish* for hospital professionals and staff. There was a proven need for a program such as mine that would develop linguistic proficiency and cultural humility so that hospital healthcare professionals and medical staff could deliver effective and respectful health care to their Hispanic patients with limited English proficiency. This textbook was written and revised during the years that I have spent teaching this certificate at Akron Children's Hospital.

Above all, I want to thank my wonderful students of *Beginning Medical Spanish I, II* and *III*, the healthcare providers and medical staff of Akron Children's Hospital. These hardworking hospital employees understood the importance of this type of program for their Spanish-speaking patients and attended classes after long work shifts, participating with enthusiasm and dedication. They offered insightful suggestions and valuable feedback that helped shape this book and the program. Richard Biering, Senior Deployment Leader at Akron Children's Hospital, was, without exception, always there when I needed him and provided enormous assistance with student recruitment and enrolment. Thank you to all of the colleagues and the administration at the University of Akron who backed this initiative specially Dean Linda Subich. I am particularly grateful to the members of the University of Akron's EX[L]Center and specially to Ian Schwarber, Matt Lee and Carolyn Behrman who not only have been huge supporters of this hospital program from its beginnings, but have created a unique and genuinely nurturing environment at the EX[L]Center where faculty initiatives are always generously recognized, highlighted and protected. It is this kind of welcoming environment that encourages creativity and allows it to flourish. A warm thanks goes to my colleague in the Spanish section, Cortney Benjamin, who was a reader of the first chapters of the manuscript and of early versions of my book proposals. She reminded me often of the importance of this project and encouraged me to continue when I most needed it.

Endless gratitude goes to family and close friends from both sides of the Atlantic—you know who you are—for your love and encouragement.

Last, but not least, I want to thank my son Niko for his tremendous help with the editing and formatting of the manuscript and for sustaining me emotionally through the process with his infinite patience and wonderful sense of humor.

Introduction

Notwithstanding the large and rapidly increasing size of a diverse US Hispanic population, there has been little increase in the number of Spanish-speaking health practitioners and supporting medical staff (Peterson-Lyer, 2008). This discrepancy contributes to linguistic and cultural difficulties and barriers for LEP (Limited English Proficiency) Hispanic patients as well as for their English-speaking healthcare providers and supporting staff members. Research has shown that now more than ever, the ability to communicate in Spanish and to develop respectful cross-cultural rapport based on an ongoing practice of self-reflection and co-learning is vital for all healthcare employees (Auerbach, 2012; Fernández et al., 2011; Martínez, 2010; Sorkin et al., 2007 and Wilson et al., 2005). Although many medical facilities do provide interpreters (physically present or remotely accessible) in order to bridge communicative barriers, they do not facilitate direct communication between healthcare employees and their patients. As a consequence, healthcare practitioners often feel excluded from the conversations and are unable to establish patient-centered care because of these language access barriers and unintentional cultural insensitivity or unawareness. Language is the means by which patients access the health delivery system and make decisions about treatments. Failure to acquire language and respectful cross-cultural relationship-building skills hinders the establishment of a trusting therapeutic alliance and of quality health care. Because of the unavailability of Spanish-speaking personnel, there is currently a strong need for a Spanish medical program that can successfully develop oral proficiency and cultural humility for professionals and staff in the health-related fields, while taking into consideration the different factors that make the attainment of these skills and sensitivity difficult.

Student audience

Beginning Medical Spanish. Oral Proficiency and Cultural Humility has been designed for current or future healthcare professionals and medical staff with minimal or no prior knowledge of Spanish who experience the difficulties of communicating linguistically and culturally with a diverse body of Spanish-speaking patients and their families. The targeted student population for this program includes any employee in the health delivery system who enters into contact with Hispanic patients and their families, from the moment they walk through the door until they leave. While the program's flexibility would allow this textbook to be used for contract training in organizations, *Beginning Medical Spanish* has been intended to be used during three 15-week college semesters or 4 college quarters at universities, colleges or community colleges that collaborate with medical schools or clinical institutions and facilities. This communicative program relies heavily on experiential, "hands-on," action learning, and as such, requires a dynamic community of interactive learners. It is not suitable as a reference handbook or as a textbook for individualized self-teaching.

Methodology

This is an oral proficiency-based program that takes into careful consideration the needs of first-time adult language learners. These learners constitute a very different student population than college undergraduate students with previous exposure to foreign languages. In many cases, this group of medical employees demonstrates a greater motivation to succeed because they understand the importance and urgency of obtaining these relationship skills in their daily delivery of health care. However, they can quickly become frustrated and intimidated with the learning process and decide to leave the program. Therefore, it is vital to take into consideration the pace of the class, the sequencing of material presented and the scheduling and timing of the courses during implementation. The learning curve for an adult learner is typically very slow during the first weeks of the initial semester, so it is critical to establish an appropriately relaxed pace with plenty of repetition and practice in the first chapters to avoid frustration and attrition. Many of the beginning programs in today's market, do not properly target adult first-time language learners as they are multiple-goal-oriented, fast-paced and introduce complex structures simultaneously without instructional support or evidence of scaffolding. *Beginning Medical Spanish* is appropriately paced and avoids the pedagogical error of presenting scripted dialogues in the first chapters that introduce complex verb structures such as: *ser, tener, estar, llamarse* and *sentir* concurrently. Grammar is introduced only when it serves oral communication and the cultural readings are in English because grammatical knowledge and reading comprehension are not the focus and do not support this oral communicative approach.

Scheduling the classes thoughtfully is another key to success for this particular population of students. Hospital employees work during the day and have to balance busy schedules on limited time. Similarly, medical students have rigorous course loads and many academic demands. For these groups, a traditional 4- or 5-day-a-week class meeting is not convenient. This program is designed around a 2-day-per-week meeting format and can accommodate the lack of available study and homework time by having students complete simple mechanical drills and activities at home, while class time becomes the experiential environment where active learning and communication takes place in an interactive way. Classes should be around an hour and a half in duration in order for students to have sufficient time to engage collaboratively and dynamically through the practice of oral activities and realistic role-plays framed in medical settings. This kind of experiential hands-on learning program makes active language acquisition possible for those who may be intimidated by learning a foreign language for the first time. It also allows students to feel confident about their skills while promoting self-refection and more positive attitudes towards their patients.

From the first day of instruction, *Beginning Medical Spanish* encourages students to comfortably engage in communicative activities ("Prácticas orales") by using simple structures that are recycled over and over again. The "Conversaciones breves" serve as communicative models that place the vocabulary or relevant grammar in an interactive context. For study time at home, the textbook offers written exercises ("Prácticas escritas"), the more mechanical and less intimidating exercises, that facilitate review and practice of relevant grammar and vocabulary away from the guidance of the instructor or the collaborative interaction with a classmate. It is not recommended that students complete the "Prácticas escritas" during class time, because this environment is intended for action learning. Since the goal is to develop oral comprehension and speaking skills, audio recordings of vocabulary and grammatical structures are available and easily accessible.

The "role-plays" are one of the most outstanding features of this program and a central component of the textbook, because they are an effective experiential activity that promotes the development of oral proficiency. Students dramatize role-plays in pairs with a partner and follow prompts written in English. They take turns practicing roles for a monitored amount of time and then they move to another partner, varying the content with each new classmate. At the end of the period, students perform the role-play in front of their class. Students enjoy listening to classmate's role-plays because they confirm that they comprehend the material and reinforce key terms and structures. Role-plays also add an atmosphere of humor and fun to the class as they allows for creativity and showcase the personalities and playfulness of some of their colleagues.

Assessments are also oral proficiency-based (except for occasional, very brief written quizzes that check control of vocabulary and verb conjugations) and consist of comprehensive role-plays that cover most of the material for that unit and recycle elements of prior ones. While they are carefully structured to reflect the skills covered, they should have open-ended components to ensure that students are not writing and memorizing a script. Images on flashcards can guide them during the preparation, practice and dramatization of these simulations. Written words in Spanish should not be included.

Student success can be measured by their performance in the final role-play. By the end of the three-semester sequence, students regularly meet the primary goals of the class and demonstrate an oral proficiency level at the Intermediate Low following the guidelines set forth by the American Council on the Teaching of Foreign Languages (ACTFL). Students at these levels can complete a series of uncomplicated tasks, respond to simple direct questions or requests for information and are able to ask or answer questions in predictable medical topics such as personal information, activities, preferences and immediate needs. They use short statements, discreet sentences and are generally understood by interlocutors accustomed to dealing with non-natives. (See: www.actfl.org/publications/guidelines-and-manuals/actfl-proficiency-guidelines-2012/english/speaking)

Layout of the text

Medical employees have busy, multilayered lives with professional and familial responsibilities. They are used to endless multitasking. This textbook is deliberately and refreshingly minimalist in its appearance. It has none of the clutter: multipaneled layouts, overprinted pages and distracting marginal annotations. This collage feeling in other texts can cause confusion or anxiety for adult learners who already feel fragmented with their busy lives. A student who opens the book can feel calm and safe knowing where to locate the section or material needed. It follows a logical organizational sequence and the different components are predictably announced by a familiar shape or icon.

Audios

The cd icon is the place holder for the audios. These are oral recordings that accompany new material in the book. They generally appear after vocabulary presentations and grammatical explanations. As one of the first obstacles to language learning is pronunciation and comprehension, students should listen often to these natural-sounding audios. It is recommended that they first listen to these very brief recordings as they read along with the printed text and that they later listen to them without using their book. Repeating what they hear out loud can be useful so that they become familiarized with the sounds.

Students may be initially overwhelmed by the medical vocabulary. They should be reminded often that most of the terms are cognates, and as such, are very similar to their English counterparts. Spanish cognates are deliberately not translated to English in the vocabulary presentations, so that students get into the habit of recognizing them and guessing their meanings.

Oral practices or "Prácticas orales"

Activities in the book that are announced with the megaphone image are oral activities meant to be practiced out loud. Some can be done at home for additional practice but most are done in class in pairs, as a preliminary interactive step to role-plays. Narration and description activities encourage students to produce language using images of medical personnel and/or patients as a springboard. The objective is for learners to describe what they see or narrate what they imagine, using discreet sentences. When done at home orally for an assignment, it is an effective tool for recycling learned material or internalizing new topics. In class, picture files elicit more spontaneous responses that can be done individually, in pairs, in group work or as a whole class. Although attempting narration and description in multiple time frames is characteristically a feature of an Intermediate High speaker, these activities are well guided, designed around a single tense, and are effective pre-role-play warm-ups for this level.

 ## *Role-plays*

This icon indicates that the activity is a role-play designed to be done by students in pairs. Role-plays are simulations that take place in a medical context. One of the primary learning outcomes of this program is be able to carry on a role-play with a classmate because it simulates the kind of interactions that medical employees are likely to have with a patient. Students are encouraged to practice their role-plays over and over again with different partners in the class, varying the content each time. Role-plays should NEVER be written out as scripts. A list of relevant vocabulary words jotted down can be consulted during the first "run" of a role-play, but books should be closed for the remainder of the practice. At the end of the class, it is important to have the students perform the practice role-plays in front of their classmates. Listening to other student's dramatizations is a useful learning tool because it improves oral comprehension and reinforces the notion that making mistakes is crucial to learning. Students should be reminded that the classroom is a safe place where everyone makes mistakes and can benefit greatly from them.

 ## Brief conversations or "Conversaciones breves"

Conversaciones breves are dialogues that follow vocabulary presentation and that frame the application of the terminology in context. They can be a reference for students when practicing role-plays or can be dramatized in class with variations of content to avoid scripted memorization.

Written homework or "Prácticas escritas"

Activities announced by the computer icon are meant to be completed at home. These written activities range from mechanical fill-in-the-blanks, to sentence-length responses to comprehension and personal questions. Even though this is an oral proficiency-based program, students need written drill-type activities to help them memorize and practice grammar structures at home before the next class meeting when they have to apply that knowledge interactively in oral communication. These exercises are deliberately designed to be simple and efficiently brief so these busy professionals are not overwhelmed by the assignments. After more than 6 years teaching at a local hospital, I have understood that current and future medical professionals and staff don't have much time outside of their busy professional schedules to invest in homework preparation. Yet, it is vital that they drill new structures and terminology when they are away from the classroom, so that they can recognize and learn new patterns. Written exercises need to be simple and brief but effective, particularly at the beginning of the program and when the instructor is not present to guide them.

See below 2 links with instructions on how to learn how to add written accent marks and Spanish punctuation to your written homework assignments.

For Mac users:
www.thoughtco.com/spanish-accents-and-punctuation-with-a-mac-3080299

For Window Users:
www.thoughtco.com/spanish-accents-and-punctuation-in-windows-3080315

The eye icon/ojo warns about exceptions or more problematic points in the grammar explanation. These sections should be studied and reviewed carefully.

Grammar explanations: Are explained in English and appear in the highlighted sections of the book. These explanations are intended to be studied carefully before homework is completed. Remind students to study the grammar before completing their written homework.

Culture or "Cultura"

Information announced by the protected globe icon is culture-based information. These brief cultural sections are sometimes followed by links that the student can quickly access for more information. Most chapters provide a robust and up-to-date bibliography for further in-depth readings on a variety of topics that may be relevant to the particular specialization or occupation of the medical employee. These references are valuable to instructors who can use the cultural content in the bibliography for class preparation and discussions. However, as cultural tools, they can only be of value if they are used as a springboard for reflection about the student's own practices, biases and the positions of power that they hold in a clinical setting with respect to their patients. A respectful and egalitarian relationship can be established when there is an empathetic challenging of the power imbalance that characterizes the traditional dynamics between a healthcare employee and a patient. Through an approach based on cultural humility and social advocacy, students can engage in an ongoing cross-cultural learning process that can foster a therapeutic alliance with Spanish-speaking patients and their families. Hispanics share a strong heritage of cultural values and beliefs that can be very different from the values in the United States; particularly with respect to family, religion/spirituality and health. Yet, individuals from diverse Hispanic communities have their own set of normative practices. Students should learn about Hispanic values and beliefs, without losing sight of the fact that each patient has a unique racial, ethnic, socioeconomic and religious/spiritual cultural identity. This multidimensional identity can be further complicated by the degree of embeddedness with their native culture or the level of acculturation in the US. The goal of these readings is not for students to strive to be "cultural experts," but rather to use the cultural information provided in the text, and in the additional readings, as fuel for self-exploration and for an ongoing production of knowledge in collaboration with the patient.

A final note on the use of the term "Hispanic" in this text. "Latino" and "Hispanic" are interchangeable terms that are used to refer to Spanish-speaking peoples from Spanish or Latin American origin. "Latinx" is a controversial gender-neutral term for "Latino/a" that has been rejected by some Hispanics as a label imposed by US academia (Hernández, 2017 and Torres, 2018). While

"Latino" refers more exclusively to people from Latin American origin or ancestry, "Hispanic" is a broader term that includes Spain. "Hispanic" is the nomenclature that has been used in the US Census since 1980 and it is the term that the government uses to encompass the broader community.

The Spanish alphabet

Letter: How the letter would be pronounced using English pronunciation:

1. A	ah
2. B	beh
3. C	seh/theh: if you are from Spain and speak Castilian Spanish (in "ce" and "ci," the "c" sounds like "s"; in "co," "ca," "cu," the "c" sounds like a "k")
4. D	deh
5. E	eh (like in pet)
6. F	ehfeh
7. G	heh (in "ge" and "gi," the "g" sounds like the English "h"; in "go," "ga," "gu," the "g" sounds like the English "g")
8. H	ache
9. I	ee (like in bee)
10. J	hota
11. K	ka
12. L	ehleh
13. M	ehmeh
14. N	ehneh
15. Ñ	ehnyeh (like in onion)
16. O	oh (sounds like the "o" in "boat")
17. P	peh
18. Q	ku (or the word from the French "coup")
19. R	ehreh
20. S	ehseh
21. T	teh
22. U	u as in (boo)
23. V	veh
24. W	doble veh
25. X	ehkees
26. Y	ee (as in bee) griega
27. Z	seta/theta if you speak Castilian Spanish

Audio I (the complete alphabet)

Listen several times and repeat.

I. Pronouncing and spelling consonants

Consonants in Spanish sound very similar to their counterparts in English. Some exceptions are:

"H" (ache) is the only silent letter in the Spanish alphabet.

"J" (hota) has a guttural sound. Pronounce this consonant as if you were clearing a throat itch.

"Ñ" (ehneh) is a nasal sound. Pronounce this consonant as you would the "ni" in onion.

When spelling words that are cognates (similar to their English counterparts), for example *profesor*, do not use double letters. Although double consonants are used frequently in English: "bb," "pp," "mm," "nn," "ff," "ss" and "tt," in Spanish they are seldom used. "LL" and "rr" are the most common double consonants.

Do not use "ph" when spelling a word with an "f" sound. In Spanish the letter "f" is used exclusively for this sound. Photograph is *fotografía*.

2. Pronouncing vowels

Vowel pronunciation is very easy in Spanish:
There are 5 vowels in the Spanish language and 5 corresponding sounds, one for each: a, e, i, o, u.

a (ah): sounds like the "a" in father, but is more open. Widen your mouth when pronouncing this vowel.

e (eh): sounds like the "e" in pet or bed.

i (ee): sounds like the "ee" in bee.

o (oh): sounds like the "o" in phone. Draw a circle O with your lips.

u (oo): sounds like the 2 "oo" in boo. Purse your lips in a tight "u," as in the English word tulle.

Audio 2 (pronouncing vowels and syllables)

Listen and repeat.

---

3. Pronouncing new words. Syllabification

To help you pronounce a new word correctly, divide it into syllables. Generally pair the consonant with the following vowel: *Ho-la*, *Lla-mo*, *Ma-ña-na*.

If there are 2 consecutive consonants divide them so they belong to different syllables: *Tar-des*, *doc-tor*.

When pronouncing 2 consecutive vowels (*ue*) pause very briefly between them as you practice the word until you become comfortable.

Días: Dí-as. (Dee-ahs) If the vowel carries a written accent mark it must be stressed when pronounced. It should be the longest syllable in the word.

Bibliography

Auerbach, Andrew. "Language Barriers and Understanding of Hospital Discharge Instructions." *Medical Care*, vol. 50, no. 4, 2012, 283–89.

DeGuzmán, María. "¡Estamos aquí!, or Being 'Latinx' at UNC-Chapel Hill." Cultural Dynamics, vol. 29, no. 3, 2017, 214–230.

Fernández, Alicia et al. "Language Barriers, Physician-Patient's Language Concordance, and Glycemic Control Among Uninsured Latinos with Diabetes: The Diabetes Study of Northern California." *Journal of General Medicine*, vol. 26, no. 2, 2011, 170–176.

Hernandez, Daniel. "The Case against Latinx." *LA Times*, December, 2017.

Martínez, Glenn A. "Language and Power in Health Care: Towards a Theory of Language Barriers among Linguistic Minorities in the US." *Reading in Language Studies: Language and Power*, vol. 2, 2010, 59–74.

Sorkin, Dara H. et al., "Providing High-Quality Care for Limited English Proficient Patients: The Importance of Language Concordance and Interpreter Use." *Journal of General Medicine*, vol. 22, 2007, 324–330.

Peterson-Lyer, Karen. "Culturally Competent Care for Latino Patients." *Markkula Center for Applied Ethics*, Santa Clara University, 1 July 2008, www.scu.edu/ethics/focus-areas/bioethics/resources/culturally-competent-care/culturally-competent-care-for-latino-patients/.

Torres, Lourdes. "Latinx." Latino Studies, vol.15, no.3, 2018, 283–285.

Wilson, Elizabeth et al., "Effect of Limited English Proficiency and Physician Language on Health Care Comprehension." *Journal of General Medicine*, vol. 20, no. 9, 2005.

Chapter 1

Greeting and addressing your patients

LEARNING OUTCOMES FOR CHAPTER 1

Oral proficiency

Students will acquire the oral communicative skills that will allow them to appropriately interact in Spanish with their patients in the following ways:

- Greet a patient according to the time of the day, their title or marital status.
- Introduce themselves using the verb (*llamarse*).
- Ask/report the patient's name using the verb (*llamarse*).
- Identify their own occupation in the medical setting.
- Address the patient (child or adult) using a culturally appropriate linguistic register.

Cultural humility

By the end of this chapter, students will understand the differences between the notions of "cultural competence" and "cultural humility." They will be able to explain the value of "cultural humility" as a self-reflective and collaborative approach to learning from their patients. Students will understand how to respond to patients with "cultural humility" when learning about:

- Greeting the patient (child or adult) using culturally appropriate body language.
- The cultural concept of *respeto* and the hierarchical cultural structures that may exist in some traditional Hispanic communities.
- Addressing patients and family members according to their age, gender and social status.
- Using the patient's last names when addressing him or her, taking into consideration the individual's preferences or level of acculturation to the US.

A. Greetings and farewells

1. Greeting

Hola	Hello	Informal greeting
Buenos días	Good morning (morning lasts until noon)	Formal greeting
Buenas tardes	Good afternoon (afternoon is from noon to dinner time, typically, 7 pm–9 pm)	Formal greeting
Buenas noches	Good evening (from 7 pm)	Formal greeting

◉ ¡OJO!

Remember that the "h" is the only silent letter in the Spanish alphabet. Do not pronounce the "h" in *hola*. Also, note that the (masculine) "o" in *buenos días* changes to a (feminine) "a" when followed by *tardes* and *noches*. This means that the noun *días* is masculine, while the nouns *tardes* and *noches* are feminine. Pronounce these greetings out loud to yourself so that you get used to saying these words properly.

2. Titles

doctor / a

señor + last name (married or single)	Mr.
don + first name	Mr.
señora (married)	Mrs.
doña + first name (married)	Mrs.
señorita (single)	Miss or Ms.

Do not capitalize *doctor(a), señor(a), don, doña* or *señorita* when followed by a name. Do capitalize when abbreviated: *Dr., Dra., Sr., Sra., D., Dña.* or *Srta.*

Source: www.thoughtco.com/spanish-abbreviations-3080289

♫ Audio 1 (greetings and titles)

Listen and repeat. It is important that you listen to these audios often. You can upload them to your cell phone and listen to them while you drive to and from work.

Cultura 1 ("cultural competence" versus "cultural humility")

Healthcare professionals and staff in the US are compelled to interact with an increasingly diverse Spanish-speaking patient population in order to establish therapeutic cross-cultural communication and relationships, reduce health disparities and increase access to quality health care. For over 2 decades, medical professionals have received training in "cultural competence" as a means of recognizing the importance of cultural diversity and developing the necessary skills to provide culturally sensitive patient care. While the origins of this concept have been traced to the social and political demands for social equality in the 60s and 70s, "cultural competence" has attained wide acceptance and has been incorporated in policies, standards and practices in the US (Chiarenza et al., 2012). As a practice, "cultural competence" claims to make cultural "experts" out of healthcare and social professionals by leading them to "master" knowledge of the cultural values, beliefs and practices of their objects of study: the patients. However, critics have questioned the validity and effectiveness of this construct by indicating that this is a self-focused approach that mimics institutional power imbalances, is paternalistic and has strong stereotyping tendencies. Against the limitations of this approach, "cultural humility" has emerged as a more ethical and respectful alternative (Tervalon and Murray-García, 1998). It is an open-minded and collaborative approach that is grounded on self-exploration and examination of one's own personal biases. The development of cultural sensitivity through humility requires students to be life-long learners through a process that involves stepping outside of their own linguistic and cultural reference-system. It involves coming to terms with the fact that one's own cultural identity and experiences can limit one's perspectives and frame the ways in which patients are perceived.

Source: https://thesocialworkpractitioner.com/2013/08/19/cultural-humility-part-i-what-is-cultural-humility/; https://socialwork.sdsu.edu/insitu/diversity/cultural-humility-a-lifelong-practice/; www.ncbi.nlm.nih.gov/pmc/articles/PMC4742464/; www.ncbi.nlm.nih.gov/pmc/articles/PMC3834043/

3. Farewells and thanks

Adiós	Goodbye
Hasta luego	See you later
Hasta pronto	See you soon
¡Muchas gracias!	Thank you
¡De nada!	You are welcome

Audio 2 (farewell)

Listen and repeat slowly. Make sure that you stress the underlined vowels.

Cultura 2 (titles and respeto)

Hispanic culture can be hierarchical to varying degrees depending on the cultural identity of the individual. When interacting with others, Hispanics may place importance on status differences determined by age, gender, occupation and socioeconomic position. Older people may expect to be treated with formality and find it respectful that the healthcare provider or staff member address them using the appropriate title or using a formal gesture, such as a handshake. In turn, the Hispanic patient or family member will often be respectful with healthcare providers since they are often considered authority figures. It is important to always thank your patient when they take leave of you: *¡Muchas gracias, señorita, señora or señor!* When they thank you, you can respond with a polite *No, gracias a usted* "No, thank you" or *De nada / No hay de qué* "You're welcome!" Depending on their background, a patient may not question a recommendation out of respect (*respeto*) or not make eye contact out of politeness. Similarly, silence can be interpreted as a sign of disagreement with the practitioner's recommendation rather than of approval. Titles are closely linked to the cultural value of *respeto*, and a provider or medical staff member should always use titles and last names when addressing a

Hispanic patient in the US. The use of titles is generally most important to older patients and women. For more traditional women, *señorita* may imply that the woman is single, a virgin and hence a reputable person. Addressing a single woman as *señora* could be potentially offensive as it could imply that she is not married and sexually active (Chong, 2002). It is important to take cues from your patients, because individuals may have varying cultural expectations depending on their level of acculturation or their ethnic, racial or socioeconomic background. Ask your patients how they would like to be addressed, and make sure that they understand that it is appropriate to ask questions or discuss a recommendation. The medical interpreter can make sure that patients understand your questions and voice their concerns even if you don't have the language yet to ask them directly.

Source: www.scu.edu/ethics/focus-areas/bioethics/resources/culturally-competent-care/culturally-competent-care-for-latino-patients/

 ## *Práctica escrita I*

Write the appropriate greeting taking into consideration the time of the day and the marital status of the person being greeted.
    Model: 2:00 pm. An adult female patient: *Buenas tardes, señora.*

1. 12:05 pm. A married female patient.
2. 4:00 pm. A male doctor.
3. 11:00 am. A female teenager.
4. 3:00 pm. A female child patient.
5. 9:00 am. The godfather of a patient.
6. 7:30 pm. A female doctor.
7. 1:00 pm. A male secretary.
8. 12:10 am. The grandfather of a patient.
9. 2:00 pm. The mother of a patient.
10. 8:00 pm. The adolescent sister of your nurse.

After you have written your greetings, say them out loud several times to yourself. Did you correctly pronounce the "o"/"a" in *buenos* / *buenas*? If you are not sure, go back and read the ¡*OJO*! section announced by the eye icon above.

B. Subject pronouns and the verb (*llamarse*)

1. Subject pronouns

Yo	I	(first person singular)
Usted	you	(second person singular)
El / ella	he / she	(third person singular)

2. The verb (llamarse)

(Yo)	Me llamo	my name is
(Usted)	Se llama	your name is
(El / ella)	Se llama	his, her name is

3. Subject pronouns and verb agreements

Subject pronouns replace noun subjects, and like nouns, they indicate who is doing the action. They determine the verb ending that will be used when conjugating or personalizing the verb.

Yo me llamo, **usted** *se llama,* **ella** *se llama*

👁 ¡OJO!

Remember that a pronoun REPLACES the noun it refers to. It does not accompany it. Note below the following 2 correct examples and the third incorrect use of the pronoun accompanied by the noun it should be replacing:

1. *La paciente se llama.* You are using the subject noun: *paciente*. (This is correct.)
2. *Ella se llama.* You have replaced *paciente* with the subject pronoun *ella*. (This is correct.)
3. *La paciente ella se llama.* You are using both the noun and the subject pronoun that replaces it, together. (This is incorrect.)

4. Sentence order in declarative sentences and in questions

In a declarative sentence, the subject (noun or pronoun) is placed first and the verb follows. This is the correct order: (S+V). The verb always follows the subject even if it is a negative verb preceded by "no".

Ella + *(no) se llama María.*
   S   V

In a question, the subject (noun or pronoun) is inverted, that is placed after your verb. This is the correct order (¿V+S?). Note the inverted question mark at the beginning of the question.

¿*Se llama* + *ella* María?
 V   S

 Práctica escrita 2

Rewrite these declarative sentences as questions:
  Model: Usted se llama don Luis. ¿Se llama usted don Luis?

       S   V

1. Ella se llama Luisa.
2. Usted se llama señorita Pérez.
3. Él se llama doctor Alejo Ascorbe Martorell.
4. Usted se llama señora Luisa Ripoll Durán.

 Práctica escrita 3

Rewrite (DO NOT ANSWER) these questions as declarative sentences:

1. ¿Se llama usted señor Lalo Sánchez?
2. ¿Me llamo yo Luisa Ripoll Buades?
3. ¿Se llama ella señorita López de Durán?
4. ¿Se llama él don Jaime?

 Práctica escrita 4

On a separate sheet of paper, complete the following sentences using the correct form of the verb (*llamarse*). Try to do this exercise after you have memorized the verb endings for this verb.

1. La doctora _____ Adela Martínez Garau.
2. El presidente del hospital _____ señor Duarte.
3. Yo _____ Dra. Luisa Rullán Espada.
4. Mi paciente _____ Juan.
5. El presidente de la universidad _____ Dr. Jonás.
6. La mamá de mi paciente_____ Alicia.

 Audio 3 (names) *verbo llamarse*

Escuchar y repetir.

Cultura 3 (names)

In the US, individuals typically have a first name, a middle name and a last name, although in the last decades using a hyphen between last names has become an increasingly popular practice among some women. In Spanish-speaking countries, most people do not have a middle name. They generally use a first name and 2 last names or surnames. The first last name is the father's paternal last name. The second is the mother's paternal last name. When a woman marries, she will replace her maternal surname with the paternal. In some traditional communities a more formal *"de"* (of) precedes the husband's paternal surname. Yet, depending on the level of acculturation to the US, the individual may anglicize his/her name to fit the American naming system and use a single last name. Children can retain the paternal last name of both parents, or accommodations can be made to fit the American system. Since all of these naming systems are "correct," a culturally respectful healthcare provider or medical staff member will always ask their patients how they prefer to be addressed or under what name the patient's appointment was made.

José Durán Nadal, for example, has 2 last names. *José* is his given name. *Durán* is his father's last name, and *Nadal* is his mother's.

Isabel Truyols Orozco also has 2 last names, following Hispanic tradition. *Truyols* is her father's last name, and *Orozco* is her mother's last name.

When *Isabel* marries, she will drop her mother's last name, *Orozco*, and add her husband's *Durán*. She will be *Isabel Truyols Durán* or *Isabel Truyols de Durán*. Her primary name is still *Truyols*.

If *José* and *Isabel* have a child, *Andrés*, his full name will be *Andrés Durán Truyols*.

Source: www.thoughtco.com/spanish-surnames-meanings-and-origins-1420795

Práctica escrita 5

Nombres y apellidos. These are the names of unmarried patients. Identify and write their father's and mother's last names or *apellidos*.

1. Antonia Buades Ferrer.
2. María Pérez Talavera.
3. Olga Fernández Salgado.

Práctica escrita 6

Nombres y apellidos. Below are the names of 2 married patients. Identify and write the last names or *apellidos*.

1. Señora Alicia González Asenjo.
2. Señora Marta Toni de Fuentes.

Práctica escrita 7

Nombres y apellidos.

1. Write your full name (*nombre completo: nombre + apellidos*) in the Hispanic tradition.
2. If you are a woman and married, write out your full name before you were married. Is there a difference?
3. If you are a man and married, write out your full name before you were married. Is there a difference?
4. Write the full name, or *nombre completo*, of each of your children.
5. Identify the last names (*apellidos*) of your *profesor(a)*.

Práctica escrita 8

Contextos. Read these brief biographical snippets about patients and their relatives. Answer the questions that follow:

1. *Nicolás* is the father of a young patient. He has 2 brothers and is from México. His mother's name is *Leti García de Ascorbe*. His father's name is *Juan Ascorbe Jiménez*. Nicolás is married to *Mirta López de Ascorbe*. Write out his full name:
2. *Ana* is a 15-year-old female patient. Her mother's name is *Matilde Talavera Marroig*. Her father is *Pepe Marroig Servera*. Write *Ana's* full name:
3. *Lucía* is the mother of a patient. She is married. Her father's name is *Javier Izquierdo Ruiz*. Her mom's name is *Juana Pascual Izquierdo*. Her husband's name is *Jaime Mora Moner*. Write *Lucia's* full name:
4. *Antonio* is married. His father's name is *Fernando Fabré Ruiz*. His mother's name is *Gloria Tous Fabré*. His wife's maiden name is *Cristina Isbert Nuñez*. Write *Antonio's* full name:

C. Introductions

I. Introductions

After an introduction, use either of these 2 expressions:

Encantado / encantada	(Enchanted)
Mucho gusto	(My pleasure)

¡OJO!

Encantada, the feminine form of *encantado*, is used when the speaker is a woman, regardless of the gender of the person she is addressing. Gender agreements are made with the person speaking, NOT with the person addressed. If a man is introduced to a woman or to another man he will say *encantado*. If a woman is introduced to another woman or a man she will say *encantada*. *Mucho gusto* is invariable. It requires no gender or number agreement.

Cultura 4 (greetings and social space)

During the first clinical encounter, the greeting may be a crucial factor that determines the success or failure of the future patient/provider relationship. A new Hispanic patient will often experience a sense of apprehension or anticipation, even fear, regarding the language and culture of the provider. Eye contact, use of titles, voice tone and gestures or physical contact are very important when greeting a new patient for the first time. One very notable cultural difference between Hispanics and North Americans is the concept of social space. In the US, professionals do not generally use physical contact when greeting a hospital colleague, a patient or a member of a patient's family. A Hispanic health professional will express more familiarity with a colleague. In many communities, he may kiss the child patient on the cheek and shake the hand of family members (Chong, 2002). After a relationship has been established, it would not be unusual for the health professional to affectionately embrace the family members.

Audio 4 (introductions) *presentaciones*

Escuchar y repetir. Listen to doctor Ribas Rojo and Miss Castillo Segura introduce themselves.

Práctica oral I

Practice introducing yourself to a male patient. Greet him and then tell him your name.

D. What is the patient's name? Requesting information

1. Yes / no questions

Remember that when asking a yes/no question, you should invert the regular sentence order of declarative sentences: (S + V) *Ella +(no) se llama*

> Yes/no questions (¿Verb + subject?):
> *¿Se llama + ella, Luisa? Sí, ella se llama Luisa.*
> *¿Se llama + la paciente, Luisa? Sí, la paciente se llama Luisa.*

2. Information questions

When an information question is asked, you are required to provide specific information in your response. You are requested specific information. To inquire about someone's name, you must use the information word *¿Cómo?* with the verb *(llamarse)*. The sentence order for an information question is the same as for a yes/no question, except that for the latter you begin the question with your information word.

> Information word + verb + subject.
> *¿Cómo + se llama + usted?* What is your name?

 Audio 5 (what is your name?) *¿cómo se llama usted?*

Escuchar y repetir.

 Conversación breve

—Buenos días, señorita.
—Buenos días, doctor.
—¿Cómo se llama usted, señorita?
—Yo me llamo Ana Parada Lared, doctor.
—Mucho gusto, doña Ana. Yo me llamo doctor Luis Silva Rosignol.
—Encantada, doctor.

 Práctica escrita 9

Complete with the correct form of the verb *(llamarse)*:

1. ¿Cómo _____ ella? Ella _____ María.
2. ¿Cómo _____ tu mamá? Ella _____ señora Luisa Rodrigo Fray.

3. ¿Cómo _____tu papá? El _____ Paco.
4. ¿Cómo _____el director de tu unidad? El _____ Dr. Pérez.
5. ¿Cómo _____el hijo menor del presidente? El _____ Baron.

Role-play 1

Imagine that you are a doctor participating at a meeting for parents who send their children to the hospital's Diabetes Camp. It is an event held at the hospital at 11 am. (Give yourself a fictitious name and identity when you are approached by your classmates posing as doctors):

> Walk around the class.
> Greet 5 "parents."
> Introduce yourself.
> Ask them for their full name.
> Write down the information.

After these 5 role-plays, introduce each of these 5 parents to the whole class.

Role-play 2

Imagine that you are attending the inauguration of a new clinic in the Dominican Republic. This is an evening event, and you are meeting staff and professionals from the clinic:

> Go around the class.
> Introduce yourself.
> Ask 5 Hispanic colleagues for their names.

After these 5 role-plays, introduce each of these 5 new colleagues to the whole class.

Práctica escrita 10

Write a very simple dialogue in Spanish between a new Hispanic adult patient who you are meeting in your office or unit one early morning and you:

> Greet her.
> Introduce yourself.
> Ask her for her name.
> Say goodbye.

E. Reporting names

1. Reporting names ellos(as)

When reporting the names of a group of people, you will use the pronouns *ellos* or *ellas* "they."

Ellos / ellas   They (third person plural)

2. Gender and ellos(as)

Use *ellos* if you are referring to an all-male group or a mixed group. Use *ellas* if you are reporting about an all-female group.

¿Cómo se llaman ellos? Ellos se llaman Juan, María y Pilar

 Audio 6 (reporting names) *¿cómo se llaman ellos / ellas?*
Escuchar y repetir.

F. Addressing children informally and adults formally

1. The informal "you" or tú

In Hispanic societies, when you address another person, you must distinguish the nature of your relationship with that person. Do you interact informally with that person? Do you address them on a first name basis? If so, then the culturally appropriate form of "you" is *tú*.

In a hospital work setting, you would use the *tú* form of "you" if you are addressing a colleague, a friend or a child patient. In some cases, if you have developed a close relationship with a patient's family member, you may also use the *tú*. This *tú* (second person informal) has its own set of endings. For (*llamarse*), the form is *te llamas*.

2. The formal "you" or usted(es)

On the other hand, if you have a formal relationship with the person and you are on a last name basis or use a title (*señor, doctor*, etc.) when addressing him / her, you must use the *usted* form. In a hospital setting, you would be likely to use the *usted* form of "you" to address a supervisor or an adult patient with whom you have a formal relationship.

You should primarily use the formal Ud. with patients (other than children / friends). Use the subject pronoun usteded for both formal and informal settings when addressing more than 1 person.

Note the difference in the following 2 questions:

¿Cómo se llama usted? (formal relationship)
¿Cómo te llamas tú? (informal relationship)

Both questions receive the same answer. *Yo me llamo....*

3. "We" or nosotros(as)

Nosotros (as) is the first person plural subject pronoun or the plural of *yo*. If you are referring to yourself and another person or persons (we), use the *nosotros / as*. Use it as a response to an *ustedes* question.

¿Cómo se llaman ustedes?
Nosotras nos llamamos Juana y Pilar.

Audio 7 (formal and informal registers)

Tú, usted(es) nosotros(as) y el verbo (llamarse).

Práctica escrita II

Write the correct subject pronoun that you would use in the following situations:

   Model: You are talking to a child: *tú*. (Since you are <u>addressing</u> the child, you must use a form of "you." In this case, you will use the informal *tú* because you are on a first name basis with a child and will generally use an informal register with him/her.)

1. You are talking <u>to</u> the director of the Heart Center.
2. You are talking <u>to</u> an older patient in emergency.
3. You are talking <u>about</u> a patient's daughter.
4. You are talking <u>about</u> 2 male doctors.
5. You are a male and you are talking <u>about</u> yourself and a female colleague.
6. You are talking <u>to</u> a 10-year-old patient in your office.
7. You are talking <u>about</u> a 10-year-old patient.
8. You are talking <u>about</u> the president of your hospital.
9. You are talking <u>about</u> yourself.
10. You are talking <u>about</u> 2 female colleagues and 1 male colleague.
11. You are a male and you are talking <u>about</u> yourself and a male colleague.
12. You are answering a question <u>addressed</u> to you.
13. You are answering a question <u>addressed</u> to you (male) and a family member (male).

Bibliography

Betancourt, Joseph R. et al. "Cultural Competence in Health Care: Emerging Frameworks and Practical Approaches." *Common Wealth Fund*, 2002.

Campinha-Bacote, Josepha. "A Model and Instrument for Addressing Cultural Competence in the Delivery of Health Care Services: A Model of Care." *Journal of Transcultural Nursing,* vol. 38, no. 3, 2002, 181–184.

Campinha-Bacote, Josepha et al. "Cultural Competemility." A Paradigm Shift in the Cultural Competence versus Cultural Humility Debate-Part 1." *Online Journal of Issues in Nursing*, vol. 23, no. 1, 2018.

Chang, E-shien et al. "Integrating Cultural Humility into Health Care Professional Education and Training." *Advances in Health Sciences Education*, vol. 17, no. 2, 2012, 269–278.

Chiarenza, Antonio et al. editors. *Inequalities in Health Care for Migrants and Ethnic Minorities.* Garant, Boston, MA, 2012.

Chong, Nilda. "Cultural Values of the Latino Patient," *The Latino Patient.* Intercultural Press, Boston, MA, 2002, 21–43.

Danso, Ransford. "Cultural Competence and Cultural Humility: A Critical Reflection on Key Cultural Diversity Concepts." *Journal of Social Work*, vol. 18, no. 4, 2016, 410–430.

Gropper, Rena C. *Culture and the Clinical Encounter. An Intercultural Sensitizer for the Health Professions.* Intercultural Press, Inc., Boston, MA, 1996.

Harris, Gai et al. "Being a 'Culturally Competent' Social Worker: Making Sense of a Murky Concept in Practice." *British Journal of Social Care*, September 21, 2010, 1–18.

Hook, Joshua N. et al. "Cultural Humility: Measuring Openness to Culturally Diverse Clients." *Journal of Counseling Psychology*, vol. 60, no. 3, 2013, 353–366.

Hook, Joshua N., et al. "Cultural Humility and Hospital Safety Culture." *Journal of Clinical Psychology in Medical Settings*, vol. 23, no. 4, 2016, 402–409.

Hook, Joshua N., et al., editors. *Cultural humility: Engaging Diverse Identities in Therapy.* Washington DC, American Psychological Association, 2017.

MacKenzie, Lauren, and Andrew Hatala. "Addressing Culture within Healthcare Settings: The Limits of Cultural Competence and the Power of Humility." *Canadian Medical Education Journal*, vol. 10, no. 1, 2019, 124–127.

Owen, Jesse, et al. "Client Perceptions of Therapists' Multicultural Orientation: Cultural (Missed) Opportunities and Cultural Humility." *Professional Psychology: Research and Practice*, vol. 47, no. 1, 2016, 30–37.

Paine, David R., et al., "Humility as a Psychotherapeutic Virtue: Spiritual, Philosophical, and Psychological Foundations." *Journal of Spirituality in Mental Health*, vol. 17, 2015, 3–25.

Tervalon, Melanie and Murray-García, Jann. "Cultural Humility versus Cultural Competence: A Critical Distinction in Defining Physician Training Outcomes in Multicultural Education." *Journal of Health Care for the Poor and Underserved*, vol. 9, no. 2, 1998, 117–125.

Van Tongeren, Daryl R., et al., "Humility." *Current Directions in Psychological Science*, vol. 28, no. 5, 2019, 463–468.

Worthington Jr., Everett. L., et al., editors. *Handbook of Humility: Theory, Research, and Applications.* New York, NY: Routledge, 2017.

Yeager, Katherine et al. "Cultural Humility: Essential Foundation for Clinical Researchers." *Applied Nursing Research*, vol. 26, no. 4, 2013, 252–256.

Creating a relationship with your patients

Getting to know them and their families

LEARNING OUTCOMES FOR CHAPTER 2

Oral proficiency

Students will acquire the oral communicative skills that will allow them to appropriately interact in Spanish with their patients in the following ways:

- Describe and elicit descriptions about members of the patient's family using verb (*tener*).
- Identify and elicit responses about a patient's age and the ages of family members with the verb (*tener*).

Cultural humility

Students will demonstrate an awareness of how to respond to patients with cultural humility when learning about the following Hispanic culturally based concepts or practices:

- The cultural concept of *familismo*.
- The cultural concept of *personalismo*.
- The importance of the extended family as a support group for the patient.
- The role of the *comadre* and *compadre* as non-biological family members.
- The underlying hierarchical structure for some Hispanic families, the traditional role of males and elderly family members in decision making with regard to health decisions and the reshaping of gender roles with acculturation.

A. The family

I. Vocabulary of the family

Los bisabuelos	great grandparents
Los abuelos	grandparents
El abuelo / la abuela	grandfather / grandmother
Los padres	parents
El padre / la madre	father / mother
El padrastro / la madrastra	stepfather / stepmother
El compadre / La comadre	godfather / godmother
El esposo / la esposa	husband / wife
El hermano / la hermana	brother / sister
El hermanastro / la hermanastra	stepbrother / stepsister
El medio hermano / la media hermana	half-brother / half-sister
El tío / la tía	uncle / aunt
El sobrino / la sobrina	nephew / niece
El primo / la prima	cousin
El hijo / la hija	son / daughter
El hijastro / La hijastra	stepson / stepdaughter
El hijo único	only child
El hijo mayor	oldest son
El hijo menor	youngest son
El mellizo / la melliza	fraternal twin
El gemelo / la gemela	identical twin
El ahijado / la ahijada	godson / goddaughter
El nieto / la nieta	grandchild
In-laws:	
El suegro / la suegra	father-in-law / mother-in-law
El cuñado / la cuñada	brother-in-law / sister-in-law
El yerno / la nuera	son-in-law / daughter-in-law

 Audio I *la familia*

 ¡OJO!

The word *padres* means "parents." *Parientes* is a false cognate. It does not mean "parents," it means "relatives." Another word for relatives in Spanish is *familiares*.

2. Gender and number of singular and collective nouns

Familia is a singular noun although it refers to a group of people. When using *La familia* as the subject of a sentence, the corresponding verb ending would be the third person singular: *La familia tiene muchos amigos.* The "number" of a noun (whether it is singular or plural) or the "gender" of a noun (whether it is masculine or feminine) can be easily determined by the "gender" and "number" of the definite article that accompanies it. For example: *el terapeuta* is a male therapist because it is preceded by the masculine *el* even if the word terapeuta ends in an "a."

3. The definite article

There are 4 definite articles in Spanish: *el*, *la*, *los*, *las*. In English there is only one form: "the."

El
La
Los
Las
          The

4. Gender and number and the definite articles

Each article marks the gender and number of the noun it accompanies.

El: (masculine singular), *La*: (feminine singular), *Los*: (masculine plural), *Las*: (feminine plural)

*For a gender mixed group, always use *los*.

5. Use and omission of the definite article

When talking *about* somebody in Spanish, use the definite article with his or her title. When *addressing* the person directly, omit the definite article.

¡Buenos días, doctora! La doctora se llama Marta Capellá Nadal.

👁 ¡OJO!

As a general rule, words ending in *a* are feminine and words ending in *o* are masculine. An exception to this general rule is the word *día*. It ends in an "a," but it is masculine: *buenos días.*

The subject pronoun *él* "he" is very similar to the definite article *el* "the." A written accent mark or *tilde* marks the difference between these 2 words.

Audio 2 (gender and number of definite articles)
género y número de los artículos definidos

Conversación breve

Nurse Luisa meets a new male patient.

—Buenos días, yo me llamo enfermera Luisa Sánchez Rodrigo. ¿Cómo se llama usted?

—Buenos días, yo me llamo Marco Girón Alvarez.

—Mucho gusto, don Marco.

—Mucho gusto, enfermera Luisa. (*Don Marco and enfermera Luisa shake hands).

—Marco, ¿tiene usted a su familia aquí hoy en el hospital con usted?

—Sí, tengo a mi esposa y a mis dos hijos.

—¿Cómo se llaman?

—Mi esposa se llama Adela Frau Álvarez y mis hijos se llaman Pablo y Olga. Tengo una familia pequeña en Akron, pero en México tengo una familia muy grande.

—¿Ah, sí? ¿Cuántos hermanos tiene usted?

—Tengo siete hermanos y dos hermanas.

—¿Y tiene usted sobrinos?

—Sí, mis dos hermanas tienen esposos e hijos. Tengo dos cuñados y cinco sobrinos.

—¡Muchas gracias por la información, don Marco!

—¡Gracias a usted!

Práctica escrita I

Género y número. Next to the family word given in the table below, write in the appropriate form of the definite article (*el, la, los, las*). Consider gender and number when selecting the article. Then, for the next 4 columns, select <u>one</u> correct category by checking the box that accurately describes the gender and number of both the article and the preceding noun:

<u>Modelo</u>: *Familia*   <u>Definite Article</u>: *La*   <u>Category</u>: Fem. Sing. X

	Definite article	Masc. sing	Fem. sing	Masc. plural	Fem. plural
Mellizas					
Madrina					
Abuelos					
Cuñada					
Hermanastra					
Primo					
Tío					
Padres					

Cultura 1 (familism)

Hispanics generally place a strong emphasis on the family. *Familismo* is the term that references the centrality of the family in an individual's life and the importance of familial ties not only with the nuclear family members, but also with the extended members and with close friends, such as the *comadre* and *compadre* (Chong, 2002). *Comadres* and *compadres* are not biological family members. They are usually close friends of the family who maintain a lifelong bond with the family and are practically members of the nuclear (or immediate) family. In some Spanish-speaking countries the term *madrina* is used instead of *comadre*. They are chosen when a child is born to participate in the infant's baptism ceremony and are considered the "second" parents. Sometimes, in the rural sector, a compadre may be chosen from a higher social status so that he may help the child's position in the future. *Compadres* are expected to help the child emotionally and financially until they become adults. In the event that both parents were to pass away, the compadres will often adopt the child (Stephenson, 2003). The construct of *familismo* for Hispanic migration can also be understood as a cultural idea that expresses the nostalgia for an idealized lost home and past. In addition, families may have a defined generational and gender-based hierarchical structure, in particular with individuals that hold traditional Hispanic values. While the elderly and the males in the family have often been the decision makers in issues of health, the process of acculturation has reshaped gender roles and Hispanic women in the US have become more independent. As a result, the decision making has become progressively more democratic (Chong, 2002). Healthcare professionals should develop sensitivity to the concept of *familismo*, to the presence of extended family and close friends in the hospital and encourage their participation in decision making when discussing illnesses and treatments.

LA FAMILIA DE LA PACIENTE PAZ FERRER FERNANDEZ

Paz is your 12-year-old patient. She suffers from type I diabetes. This is her family tree:

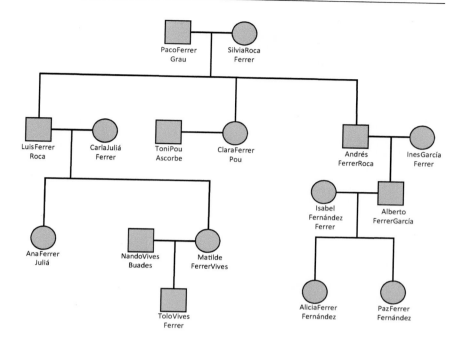

Práctica escrita 2

Preguntas de comprensión. Consult the family tree and respond to these questions with full answers. Use the appropriate subject pronouns (*él, ella, ellos o ellas*) to start your answer.

    Modelo: ¿Cómo se llaman <u>los padres de Alberto</u>? <u>Ellos</u> se llaman…

1. ¿Cómo se llaman los padres de Paz?
2. ¿Cómo se llama la hermana gemela de Paz?
3. ¿Cómo se llaman los tíos de Alberto?
4. ¿Tiene (*tener*: "to have") primos Alberto?
5. ¿Cuántos hermanos tiene el abuelo de Paz?
6. ¿Tiene bisabuela Paz?

Práctica escrita 3

Conversación con una paciente. Imagine that you are a 39-year-old female patient and the nurse asks you the following information about the names of family members. Answer in full sentences. Start the sentence with the correct subject pronoun (*él, ella, ellos o ellas*):

1. ¿Cómo se llaman sus padres?
2. ¿Cómo se llama su esposo/a?

3. ¿Cómo se llaman los hermanos de su esposo?
4. ¿Cómo se llama su hermano/a menor? mayor?
5. ¿Cómo se llama su suegro?

Práctica oral I

Ask your child patient 5 questions about their family members.

Role-play I

You are a nurse and are meeting a 13-year-old Hispanic patient for the first time:

Greet the patient appropriately
Introduce yourself.
Ask her for her name.
Ask her for her parent's names.
Ask her for her sibling's names.
Thank her.
Say goodbye.

Role-play 2

It is 8:00 am, you are a doctor, and you are meeting the 29-year-old Hispanic mother of an infant for the first time:

Greet the mother of the patient appropriately.
Introduce yourself.
Ask her for her name. (*Remember that it is culturally appropriate to shake hands when greeting or taking leave of a patient.)
Ask her for her husband's name.
Ask her for her child's name.
Thank her.
Say goodbye.

B. Possession and (*tener*) with the family

I. The verb (tener)

The verb (*tener*) "to have" is used in Spanish to express possession. Use (*tener*) to talk about family members that you have or don't have. If you don't have cousins or children, for example, use: *no tengo*:

Tengo tres hijos (I have 3 children). *Yo no tengo esposo* (I don't have a husband).

(Tener)

Yo tengo *Nosotros / as tenemos*

Tú tienes

El, ella, usted tiene *Ustedes tienen*

2. Counting family members

The numbers from 1 to 12

Uno (un / a)	1	*Siete*	7
Dos	2	*Ocho*	8
Tres	3	*Nueve*	9
Cuatro	4	*Diez*	10
Cinco	5	*Once*	11
Seis	6	*Doce*	12

 ¡OJO!

When simply counting numbers use *uno* with an o. When counting people or things, use *un* or *una* to signal the gender of the person, place or thing that you are counting:

Uno, *dos, tres*
Una *enfermera*
Un *enfermero*

 ### Audio 3 el verbo (tener)

 ### Cultura 2 (Personalismo)

Personalismo is a Hispanic culturally based concept that points to the value placed on social relationships. *Personalismo* can be illustrated in the ways in which Hispanics greet and take leave of one another by hugging or shaking hands and in their demonstrations of emotional and physical warmth (Stephenson, 2003). While the level of *personalismo* may vary with the individual depending on their level of acculturation in the US, research has theorized that one of the factors that may impact the Hispanic health paradox (low mortality and better health despite many barriers to health care) is in fact the strong social support that comes from the interconnectedness of these relationships. Talking about a patient's family is not only an ice breaker, but can help build a social and therapeutic relationship with patients.

Source: www.huffingtonpost.com/2013/01/24/hispanic-paradox-latinos-live-longer_n_2543060.html

 Audio 4 los números (1–12)

 Práctica escrita 4

La familia de Paz. Go back to the family tree of your patient Paz and answer these questions using the verb (*tener*) and the appropriate number. (Notice that when asking about quantity the question word *¿Cuántos / as?* can have a masculine or a feminine form depending on the gender of what you are counting):

1. ¿Tienen hijos Clara y Toni?
2. ¿Tiene una nieta Andrés?
3. ¿Tiene esposa Alberto? ¿Cómo se llama ella?
4. ¿Cómo se llama la nieta de Paco que (that) tiene un hijo?
5. ¿Cuántos (How many) cuñados tiene Luis? ¿Cómo se llaman?
6. ¿Cuántas primas tiene Ana? ¿Cómo se llaman?
7. ¿Cuántos sobrinos tiene Clara

 Práctica oral 2

Circular por la clase y escribir el nombre de la persona que responda afirmativamente. Circulate around the classroom and write the name of the person who answers affirmatively to your question. Remember to ask *¿cómo te llamas?* if you don't know their first name and *¿cómo se escribe?* if you don't know how to spell it:

Pregunta   Nombre del estudiante

1. ¿Tienes cuatro hermanos?   _____
2. ¿Tienes una familia grande?   _____

3. ¿Tienes una familia pequeña?   _____
4. ¿Tienes una suegra?   _____
5. ¿Tienes un padrastro?   _____
6. ¿Tienes dos nietas?   _____
7. ¿Tienes tres hijos?   _____
8. ¿Tienes cinco tías?   _____
9. ¿Tienes madrina?   _____
10. ¿Tienen tus hijos, madrastra?   _____
11. ¿Tienes gemelos?   _____
12. ¿Tienes esposo/a?   _____
13. ¿Tienes un ahijado?   _____
14. ¿Tienes un compadre?   _____

Reportar. As a follow-up, you will hear questions about your classmates. *¿Quién* ("who") *en la clase tiene 4 hermanos?* Provide the person's name in a full answer. If nobody answered affirmatively to a question, then say *Nadie en la clase tiene 4 hermanos.*

Práctica escrita 5

Los miembros de la familia. Answer with the logical member of the family:
    <u>Modelo</u>: *La madre de mi madre es* **mi: abuela.** (my grandmother)

1. El padre de mi padre es **mi:**
2. Los hijos de mi madre son **mis:**
3. La hija de mi tía es **mi:**
4. Los hijos de mi hijo son **mis:**
5. El esposo de mi madre es **mi:**
6. La madre de mi sobrino es **mi:**
7. La madre de mi esposo es **mi:**
8. El padre de mi madre es **mi:**
9. La hija de mi madre y mi padrastro es **mi:**
10. La esposa de mi hijo es **mi:**

Práctica escrita 6

Posesivos y género. Now go back to the previous *práctica* and check your answers. If the preceding word for "my" was singular (*mi*), then make sure that the family member is singular (*mi hermano, tía, padre,* etc.). If the word for "my" was plural (*mis*), the family term should also be plural and should end with an "s" (*mis hermanos, tíos, padres,* etc.):

C. Possession and possessive adjectives

I. Possessive adjectives

Possession can be indicated by using the verb *tener*: "I have a sister" or by using the possessive adjective my: "My sister."

2. Gender and number

There are 4 possessive adjectives. Each one signals the gender and/or number of what is possessed:

Mi/mis	my	*Nuestro/a/os/as*	our
Tu/tus	your (informal)		
Su/sus	your (formal), his, her	*Su/sus*	you,(plural) their

¡OJO!

1. Remember that, as adjectives, the possessives describe (in gender and number) what is possessed, NOT the possessor. Note the example below:
   *María tiene **dos** hermanos. **Sus** hermanos gemelos* (her twin brothers) *tienen 6 años.*
   In this case, *sus* is the appropriate plural possessive adjective because what is "possessed" (her brothers) is plural, even though María is a singular subject.
2. In English, the apostrophe is also used to express possession. For example: "My brother's wife" (or "The wife of my brother"). In Spanish, there is no such use of the apostrophe to express possession. You must use *de* ("of") to express that relationship. *"La esposa de mi hermano."*

Práctica escrita 7

Apostrophes. Write the correct sentence in Spanish with the substitute *de* for the English apostrophe and the appropriate possessive adjective. (Re-read number 2 above in ¡OJO! for further clarification.)
   Modelo. My brother's wife. *La esposa **de** mi hermano.*

1. My cousin's children.
2. Our sister's doctor.
3. Your (formal) patient's family.
4. Their grandmother's nephew.
5. My godson's parents-in-law.
6. My children's cousins.
7. His uncle's niece.
8. My colleague's (*colega*) professor.
9. Your (informal) nurse's sister-in-law.
10. The parents of her patients.

*Now go back, review your answers and double check that you have a *de* before the possessive adjectives, in each sentence.

Práctica escrita 8

Los adjetivos posesivos. Indicate that each person "possesses" the corresponding items/people. *Completar con el adjetivo posesivo correcto*:

1. Yo tengo _____ libro de español.
2. Ella tiene _____ libros.
3. Mi paciente tiene una abuela. _____ abuela se llama Juana.
4. El doctor tiene un paciente. _____ paciente no habla español.
5. Los enfermeros no tienen _____ medicinas en casa.
6. Nosotros hablamos con _____ recepcionista.
7. Los pediatras hablan con _____ secretarias.
8. Ustedes invitan a _____ colegas a la conferencia.

Role-play 3

You are a nurse and you are interviewing an adult patient (formally):

> Greet him/her formally.
> Introduce yourself.
> Ask for his/her name.
> Give the appropriate cultural response. (*Remember that it is culturally appropriate to shake hands with your adult patients.)

Ask these questions about your patient's family by providing the appropriate possessive adjective. Before you start, complete the questionnaire below. Then proceed with the interview:

1. ¿Cómo se llama ___ madre?
2. ¿Cómo se llama ___ padre?
3. ¿Cómo se llama ___ hermano/a mayor, hermano menor?
4. ¿Cómo se llaman ___ hijos
5. ¿Cómo se llama ___ hijastro?
6. ¿Cómo se llaman ___ ahijados?
7. ¿Cómo se llaman ___ sobrinos?
8. ¿Cómo se llama ___ compadre?
9. ¿Cómo se llama ___ esposo/esposa?
10. ¿Cómo se llama ___ suegro/a?

After the *entrevista* or "interview," introduce your patient to your colleagues (*Mi paciente se llama*) and tell them about their families. (*Su madre se llama…*)

Role-play 4

You are interviewing a child patient (informally):

> Greet him/her informally.
> Introduce yourself.
> Ask for his/her name.
> Give an appropriate cultural response.

Ask these questions about your patient's family by providing the appropriate possessive adjective. Before you start, complete the questionnaire below. Then proceed with the interview:

1. ¿Cómo se llama ___ madre?
2. ¿Cómo se llama ___ padre?
3. ¿Cómo se llama ___ hermano/a mayor, hermano menor?
4. ¿Cómo se llaman ___ hijos
5. ¿Cómo se llama ___ padrastro?
6. ¿Cómo se llama ___ madrastra?
7. ¿Cómo se llaman ___ abuelos?
8. ¿Cómo se llaman ___ abuelas?
9. ¿Cómo se llaman ___ primos?
10. ¿Cómo se llaman ___ vecinos?

After the *entrevista*, introduce your patient to your colleagues (*mi paciente se llama*) and tell them about their families (*Su madre se llama*).

D. Inquiring about a patient's age. The numbers from 13 to 90

I. Vocabulary. The numbers

13 trece	*21 veintiuno (veinte y uno)*
14 catorce	*22 veintidós (veinte y dos)*
15 quince	*23 veintitrés (veinte y tres)*
16 dieciséis (diez y seis)	*24 veinticuatro (veinte y cuatro)*
17 diecisiete (diez y siete)	*25 veinticinco (veinte y cinco)*
18 dieciocho (diez y ocho)	*26 veintiséis (veinte y seis)*
19 diecinueve (diez y nueve)	*27 veintisiete (veinte y siete)*
20 veinte	*28 veintiocho (veinte y ocho)*
	29 veintinueve (veinte y nueve)

30 treinta, 40 cuarenta, 50 cincuenta, 60, sesenta, 70 setenta, 80 ochenta y 90 noventa

From 16 to 29, you have a choice to either write the number as 1 word by inserting an *i* or as 2 words by separating with a *y*. After 29, you must always use a *y* between tens and units.

---

2. Age

The verb (*tener*) means "to have" and it is used to talk about age. Always include the word *años* "years" in your answer when talking about your age to avoid confusion:

> *Yo tengo 15 primos.*   *Yo tengo 15 años.*

 ¡OJO!

Pronounce the number *vein-te* carefully. It should sound like the word "vein" in English. Avoid *switching the "ei" to "ie."*

 Audio 5 los números (13–90)

 Práctica escrita 9

¿Cuántos años tienen sus pacientes y sus familiares? Consult the birthdates written below by your assistant and write the age of your patients or their relatives using full answers. Do not use digits, but rather spell all numbers for extra practice:

  Modelo: Su paciente María: 2011. Mi paciente María tiene _____ años.

1. Pablo, el padre de María: 1992.
2. La señora Pou Isbert, la comadre de Pablo: 1993.
3. Tu paciente Isabel: 2011.
4. José, el hermano menor de Isabel: 2013.
5. La señora Sanchez León, la madre de Isabel: 1985.
6. La señora Lucía, la abuela de Isabel: 1966.
7. El bisabuelo de Isabel: 1932.

 Práctica escrita 10

Preguntas al paciente. You are a 43-year-old female patient and you are chatting with the nurse about your family members, after a medical appointment. Answer in full sentences with your personal information:

1. ¿Cuántos hermanos tiene usted?
2. ¿Cuántos primos maternos tiene usted?

3. ¿Cuántos hijos tiene usted? ¿Cuántos años tienen ellos?
4. ¿Cuántos hijos tiene su hermano?
5. ¿Cuántos tíos paternos tiene usted?
6. ¿Cuántos hermanos tiene su padre?
7. ¿Cuántas hermanas tiene su madre?
8. ¿Cuántos sobrinos tiene usted?

 ## Role-play 5

You are conversing formally with the 32-year-old mother of a child patient. Each time you practice this role-play with a classmate vary the content. (*Remember to always thank the patient for her responses with a *¡Muchas gracias, señorita, señora* or *señor!* If they thank you, you can respond with a thank you back: *¡Gracias a usted!* or by saying "You are welcome!": *¡de nada!* or *¡no hay de qué!*)

> Greet her.
> Introduce yourself.
> Ask for her name. (*Remember that it is culturally appropriate to shake hands when meeting or taking leave of a patient.)
> Ask for her age.
> Ask for the name of the relative accompanying her (could be a spouse, another family member or a godparent).
> Ask for the name or age of her spouse (if he is not accompanying her).
> Ask how many children she has.
> Ask for their names.
> Find out her age and the age of her children.
> Ask any other questions you would like about other family members.
> Say goodbye.

Bibliography

Chong, Nilda. "Cultural Values of the Latino Patient," *The Latino Patient.* Intercultural Press, 2002, pp. 21–43.

Crouch, Edward C. *Mexicans & Americans: Cracking the Cultural Code.* Brealey Publishing, 2004.

Flores, Glen. "Culture and the Patient-Physician Relationship: Achieving Cultural Competency in Health Care." *The Journal of Pediatrics*, vol. 136, no. 1, 2000, 14–23.

Germán, Miguelina et al. "Familism Values as a Protective Factor for Mexican-Origin Adolescents Exposed to Deviant Peers." *The Journal of Early Adolescence*, vol. 29, no. 1, 2009, 16–42.

Juckett, Gregory. "Caring for Latino Patients." *American Family Physician*, vol. 87, no. 1, 2013, 48–54.

Smith-Morris, Carolyn et al. "An Anthropology of Familismo: On Narratives and Description of Mexican/Immigrants." *Hispanic Journal of Behavioral Sciences*, vol. 31, no. 11, 2013, 35–60.

Stephenson, Skye. *Understanding Spanish-Speaking South Americans: Bridging Hemispheres.* Intercultural Press, 2003.

Identifying and describing people and places in the hospital

LEARNING OUTCOMES FOR CHAPTER 3

Oral proficiency

Students will acquire the oral communicative skills that will allow them to appropriately interact in Spanish with their patients in the following ways:

- Describe and elicit descriptions of people using adjectives and the verb (*ser*).
- Introduce colleagues from the hospital and identify their specialties or occupations to patients.
- Identify rooms, units, centers, departments and public spaces in the hospital to patients.

Cultural humility

Students will demonstrate an awareness of how to respond to patients with cultural humility when learning about the following Hispanic culturally based concepts or practices that may vary depending on the cultural identity of the individual or their level of acculturation to the US:

- The culturally based concept of the *botánica* or *hierbería/yerbería* rather than the pharmacy and the expectations of prescribed medication without a prescription.
- The culturally based practice of self-treatment when medication is not immediately available.

A. Identifying and describing with the verb (ser)

I. The verb (ser) ¿Quién es? ¿Cómo es?

Ser "to be" is used in Spanish to identify and describe. When identifying or describing physical attributes or personality traits of patients and their family members use (*ser*):

> *¿Quiénes son? Ellas son mis hermanas.* (You have been asked to identify)

When inquiring about someone's physical appearance or character traits use the question: *¿Cómo es?*

> *¿Cómo es su hermana? Ella es extrovertida.* (You are offering a description)

(Ser)	
Yo soy	*Nosotros/as somos*
Tú eres	
El, ella, usted es	*Ellos, ellas, ustedes son*

 Audio I el verbo (ser)

 Práctica escrita I

¿Cómo es/son?/¿Quién(es) es/son? Determine if the reply is providing an identification or a description and use a form of *¿Quién(es) es/son)?* or *¿Cómo es/son?* to provide the question that was asked:

Modelo: *Son los doctores de mi hijo.   ¿Quiénes son?*

1. Mi paciente es tímida:
2. El niño es muy agresivo:
3. Son los padres de mi paciente:
4. Es la terapeuta:
5. Las doctoras son muy activas:
6. Es la comadre de la madre de mi paciente:

 Práctica escrita 2

¿Cómo es la familia de mi paciente, Paz? Completar las descripciones con la forma correcta del verbo (ser):

1. La familia de mi paciente Paz _____ grande.
2. Su hermana Alicia no _____ mayor. Ella no _____ menor. Ella _____ su gemela.

3. Tolo_____ hijo único. No tiene hermanos. El _____ depresivo.
4. La hermana de su abuelo Andrés _____ Clara. Ella _____ muy equilibrada.
5. Carla _____ su cuñada.
6. Las sobrinas de Andrés _____ Ana y Matilde.
7. Los bisabuelos de Paz _____ Paco y Silvia. Ellos _____ muy viejos pero _____ activos

B. Describing people in a hospital. Descriptive adjectives

I. Vocabulary. Descriptive adjectives

Adjectives describe people, places or things (nouns). Below are lists of adjectives that describe personality and physical characteristics. They are always introduced in the masculine form which is the "default" form in Spanish:

Personalidad:

Activo=atlético / pasivo
Apático: letárgico /
  enérgico.
Atrasado / Adelantado
Cooperativo / no colaborador
Cómico / serio
Depresivo=melancólico / alegre
Educado / maleducado
Equilibrado / bipolar
Estudioso=trabajador / flojo
Generoso / tacaño
Interesante / aburrido
Introvertido / extrovertido
Liberal / conservador
Maduro / inmaduro
Nervioso: ansioso: hiperactivo /
Relajado: tranquilo
Responsable / irresponsable.
Problemático
Sedentario
Sensible / insensible
Simpático / antipático
Tímido / agresivo

Físico:

autista
alérgico, anémico, anoréxico,
  artrítico, cólico, diabético
alto / bajo/mediano
atractivo / feo
débil / fuerte
enfermizo / sano
esquizofrénico, histérico
gordo/obeso / flaco: delgado
grande / pequeño
joven / viejo=mayor
rubio / moreno / pelirrojo / calvo

2. Agreement and descriptive adjectives

Adjectives must agree in gender (masculine/feminine) and number (singular/plural) with the nouns, in this case people, that they describe. For example, a feminine adjective cannot be used to describe a male patient nor a singular adjective to describe a group of patients. Because there must be an agreement between a noun and the adjectives that describes it, most adjectives of description in Spanish have different forms to mark the gender and number of the person(s) described.

o = masculine singular, *a* = feminine singular, *os* = masculine plural, *as* = feminine plural

3. Gender forms

When the masculine singular form of an adjective ends in an *o*, the feminine singular form ends in an *a*:

El es introvertido. Ella es introvertida.

When the masculine singular form of an adjective ends in an *e*, the feminine singular will also end in an *e*:

El es grande. Ella es grande.

When the masculine singular form ends in a consonant, the feminine will also share that ending:

El es joven. Ella es joven.   *El es liberal. Ella es liberal.*

4. Number

If the singular adjective ends in a vowel, add an s to make it plural

Ellos son introvertidos. Ellas son introvertidas.

If the adjective ends in a consonant, add an *es* to make it plural:

Ellos son jóvenes.

👁 ¡OJO!

For adjectives that end in *or* (*conservador* or *trabajador*) the feminine singular form is *ora*. *Simpático* is a *falso cognado* or "false cognate." It does not mean "sympathetic," but rather "friendly." *Sensible* is also a *falso cognado*. It does not mean "sensible" (*con / sin sentido común*), but rather "sensitive."

Conversación breve

Doctor Gómez talks to doña Luisa about her daughter Juanita.

—¿Cómo se llama su hija, doña Luisa?
—Mi hija se llama Juanita, doctor.
—¿Cuántos años tiene Juanita?
—Tiene diez años.
—¿Diez años? ¡Es muy pequeña y flaca, doña Luisa!
—Sí, tiene muchos problemas. Es anoréxica y depresiva.
—¿Tiene amigas en la escuela?
—No, doctor. Es muy introvertida.

Audio 2 los adjetivos

Práctica oral I (en clase)

Entrevistas. La descripción de su paciente. You are interviewing a 19-year-old female patient (you will have to produce the feminine form of the adjectives given below, as the default form is always masculine in Spanish):

1. ¿Eres introvertido o extrovertido?
2. ¿Eres liberal o conservador?
3. ¿Eres cómico o serio?
4. ¿Eres generoso o tacaño?
5. ¿Eres trabajador o flojo?
6. ¿Eres diabético?
7. ¿Eres activo o pasivo?
8. ¿Eres responsable o irresponsable?
9. ¿Eres ansioso o tranquilo?
10. ¿Eres anémico?

Reportar. You are talking about your patient to a colleague. Report the information from your questions.

Práctica escrita 3

La familia. ¿Cómo es? (You are a 40-year-old male patient who is chatting with his cardiologist about his family). Contestar con una frase completa y un adjetivo de descripción física de la lista:

1. ¿Cómo es su esposa?
2. ¿Cómo son sus hijos?

3. ¿Cómo es su cuñada?
4. ¿Cómo es su suegra?
5. ¿Cómo es su comadre?
6. ¿Cómo es su hermano/a?
7. (Otra pregunta).

 Role-play I

Conversación informal. Mis suegros. You are chatting with a 25-year-old female patient who just announced that she got married. Ask your patient about his or her in-laws and their personality traits and physical characteristics. Then talk briefly about your in-laws. Use vocabulary of the family, descriptive adjectives and adjectives of personality.

C. Identifying your colleagues

I. Vocabulary. Professionals at your hospital

El asistente (dental, médico/técnico/al director)

El cardiólogo	**El/la analista*
El cirujano	*El/la dentista*
El diabetólogo/endocrinólogo	*El/la especialista*
El director	*El/la internista*
El empleado	*El/la nutricionista*
El enfermero	*El/la oculista*
El farmacéutico	*El/la ortopeda*
El ginecólogo	*El/la pediatra*
El médico de cabecera	*El/la (p)siquiatra*
El nefrólogo	*El/la recepcionista*
El (p)sicólogo	*El/la terapeuta*
El radiólogo	
El secretario	
El supervisor	
El trabajador social	
El urólogo	
El voluntario	

¡OJO!

The nouns marked with an asterisk on the right column above are unusual because the masculine form ends in an *a*, rather than *o*. This means that both the masculine and feminine forms share the same ending. To specify the gender of a male or female professional include the gender correct form of the definite article *(el / la)*.

Contrast:

El radiólogo / la radióloga   El pediatra / la pediatra

 Audio 3 *los profesionales*

 Práctica escrita 4

Género y número de las profesiones. Completar con la forma correcta y el artículo correcto:

Modelo. *Especialista* (femenino plural): ***Las especialistas.***

1. Dentista (masculino plural):
2. Cirujano (femenino singular):
3. Recepcionista (masculino singular):
4. Terapeuta (masculino plural):
5. Supervisor (femenino plural):
6. Enfermero (femenino plural):
7. Pediatra (masculino plural):
8. Enfermero (masculino singular):
9. Nutricionista (masculino plural):
10. Ortopeda (femenino singular):

 Práctica escrita 5

Identificar las profesiones de sus colegas y completar con la forma correcta del verbo (ser):

1. Ella _____ la pediatra.
2. Nosotros _____ los enfermeros del hospital.
3. Usted _____ el especialista.

4. Ellas _____ las supervisoras.
5. ¿_____ ustedes los ginecólogos?
6. Tú _____ la nefróloga. ¿Verdad?
7. Yo no _____ el médico. _____la recepcionista.

Role-play 2

¿Cuál es tu profesión en el hospital? You are a cardiologist and meet a new pediatrician in the cafeteria at lunch time. Hold an informal conversation. (Vary this content with each classmate. Provide different specialties or professions):

> Greet him/her.
> Introduce yourself (*nombres y apellidos completos*).
> Identify your profession.
> Ask about his/her profession (*¿Cuál es tu profesión en el hospital*).
> Ask 3 yes/no questions about his/her personality.
> Ask 3 family questions.
> Say goodbye.

Role-play 3

Hablando de un paciente. You meet up with a colleague, an endocrinologist who specializes in diabetes, (diabetólogo) in the cafeteria for breakfast. Talk about the new "difficult" young pre-teen male patient that you saw him with earlier. (Vary this content with each classmate. Provide different illnesses: *esquizofrénico, histérico, hiperactivo y autista*:)

> Greet your colleague.
> Ask him for the name of his patient.
> Ask him if his patient is diabetic. Use other related adjectives to ask about his physical identity.
> Ask him about the patient's family history with diabetes (mother, father, siblings).
> Ask 3 questions about his young patient's personality.
> Say goodbye.

D. Stating existence with the verb (*haber*)

I. The verb (haber)

(*Haber*) is used to talk about the existence of people or things in a particular place. It is a special verb because it is not personalized or conjugated like other verbs. It has one verb form only (it is invariable): *(no) hay*

Hay un hospital de niños en Akron. No hay pediatras en la clase.

2. Subject pronouns and the verb (haber)

Never use a pronoun (*yo, tú, él, ella, usted, nosotros, ustedes, ellos, ellas*) with this verb. The subject is already built-in to the verb form ("there is/are").

3. Pronunciation

Remember that the "h" is silent in Spanish. Pronounce *hay* like the English word "eye."

Práctica oral 2

¿Quién hay en la clase de español? Circular por el salón de clases e identificar a los compañeros. Circulate around the classroom and ask your classmates/colleagues about their identities as family members and as professionals in the hospital. Tally the yes answers and then report your findings to the class about the population using *"hay"* or *"no hay"*:

A.

    1. ¿Eres abuelo?
    2. ¿Eres profesor?
    3. ¿Eres enfermero?
    4. ¿Eres madre?
    5. ¿Eres padre?
    6. ¿Eres gemelo?
    7. ¿Eres doctor?
    8. ¿Eres supervisora?
    9. ¿Eres pediatra?
    10. ¿Eres empleado del hospital?
    11. ¿Eres recepcionista?

B.

    1. ¿Hay un abuelo en la clase?
    2. ¿Hay una profesora espanola en la clase?
    3. ¿Cuántas enfermeras hay en la clase?

4. ¿Cuántas madres hay en la clase?
5. ¿Cuántos padres hay en la clase?
6. ¿Cuántos gemelos hay en la clase?
7. ¿Cuántos doctores hay en la clase?
8. ¿Cuántos supervisores hay en la clase?
9. ¿Cuántos empleados del hospital hay en la clase?
10. ¿Cuántos recepcionistas hay en la clase?
11. ¿Cuántos pediatras hay en la clase?

E. Identifying places in the hospital

¿Hay una sala de espera en tu hospital?, ¿en el edificio Principal?,
¿en qué edificio?

I. Rooms and units

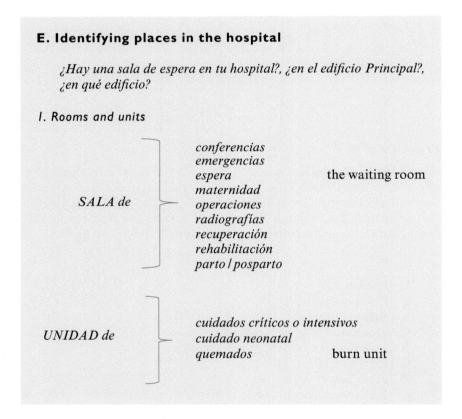

SALA de — *conferencias*
emergencias
espera   the waiting room
maternidad
operaciones
radiografías
recuperación
rehabilitación
parto / posparto

UNIDAD de — *cuidados críticos o intensivos*
cuidado neonatal
quemados   burn unit

Audio 4 salas y unidades en tu hospital

2. Departments and centers

	cirugía surgery
	corazón / cardiología
	gerontología
	nefrología
DEPARTAMENTOS de o	*neurología*
CENTROS de	*oncología*
	ortopedia
	patología
	recursos humanos
	respiración
	terapia física
	urología

 Audio 5 departamentos o centros en tu hospital

 Práctica escrita 6

¿Cómo es tu hospital? Contestar con descripciones:

1. ¿Hay un departamento o centro de cardiología en tu hospital?
2. ¿Cuántas salas de recuperación hay?
3. ¿Hay una unidad de quemados en tu edificio?
4. ¿En qué edificios hay salas de cuidados críticos?
5. ¿Es grande la sala de emergencias de tu hospital?
6. ¿Es atractiva la sala de espera en tu unidad?
7. ¿Hay una sala de parto en la sala de maternidad? ¿de posparto?
8. ¿En qué *pisos* (floors) hay salas de conferencias?

 Práctica escrita 7

Descripción y narración. ¿Quiénes son y cómo son? Describe and write the scene below using what you see in the image below and your imagination. Only use the vocabulary and the verbs we have learned so far.

1. (Identificación de ella: Nombre, apellidos y profesión)
2. (Edad de ella)
3. (Descripción física de ella)
4. (Descripción personalidad de ella)

5. (Identificación de él)
6. (Edad de él)
7. (Descripción física de él)
8. (Descripción personalidad de él)
9. (Identificación del lugar en el hospital)

 Práctica escrita 8

Descripción y narración. ¿Quiénes son y cómo son? Describe and write the scene below using what you see in the image and your imagination. Follow the template of questions from Práctica 7.

3. Vocabulary. Public places in the hospital

MASCULINOS

El aparcacoches	the valet parking
El ascensor amarillo, anaranjado, gris, verde	the yellow, orange, gray, green elevator
El banco de sangre	blood bank
El edificio	the building
El aparcamiento	the parking
El lavabo / el servicio	the restroom
El pasillo	the hallways
El piso	floor
El puente	the bridge

El quiosco
El restaurante

FEMENINOS

La cafetería	
La capilla	the chapel
La entrada	the entrance
de empleados o de visitantes	
La entrada principal	
La estación de enfermeras	
La farmacia	
La oficina administrativa	
La recepción	
La salida	the exit
La tienda de regalos	the gift shop
Las escaleras	the stairs
Las escaleras mecánicas	

¡OJO!

The word "location" does not have a cognate in Spanish even though words ending in "tion" in English, frequently have a cognate in Spanish that end in *ción*. The correct term for "location" in Spanish is *lugar* or *ubicación*.

Audio 6 (public places in the hospital) *lugares en el hospital*

Cultura I (*botánicas o hierberías*)

In many Hispanic countries, patients can buy their medication at the local pharmacy without a doctor's prescription. In the US, they make seek local

Hispanic healers to provide them with herbs or alternative medications at the local *botánicas* or *hierberías / yerberías* when they are not able to obtain them at the pharmacy because they don't have a prescription. Sometimes they have medication sent to them from their native communities (Hollingshead et al., 2016). It is very important to ask patients what medications they are using or giving their children and where they are obtaining them (Young, 2009). An accepting and non-judgmental attitude from the health provider will contribute to a patient's willingness to share information (Shelley, 2009).

Práctica escrita 9

Preguntas personales. Conteste a las preguntas con frases completas:

1. ¿Hay un quiosco en su edificio?
2. ¿Hay una unidad de cuidado neonatal en su hospital?
3. ¿Hay un café Starbucks en su hospital?
4. ¿Hay un banco de sangre en su hospital?
5. ¿Hay un aparcacoches en su hospital?
6. ¿Cuántas entradas hay en el edificio principal?
7. ¿Cuántos edificios hay en su hospital?
8. ¿Cuántos pisos hay en su edificio?
9. ¿Cuántos pisos hay en el edificio principal?
10. ¿Hay un departamento de radiología en su piso o clínica?
11. ¿Hay una unidad de quemados en su hospital?
12. ¿En qué piso hay servicios?
13. ¿En qué piso hay laboratorios?

Bibliography

Hollingshead, Nicole A. et al. "The Pain Experience of Hispanic Americans: A Critical Literature Review and Conceptual Model." *The Journal of Pain: Official Journal of the American Pain Society*, vol. 17, no. 5, 2016, 513–528.

Juckett, Gregory. "Caring for Latino Patients." *American Family Physician*, vol. 87, no. 1, 2013, 48–54.

Lopez, Rebecca. "Use of Alternative Folk Medicine by Mexican American Woman." *Journal of Immigrant Health*, vol. 7, no. 1, 2005, 23–31.

Shelley, Brian M. "They Don't Ask Me So I Don't Tell Them: Patient–Clinician Communication about Traditional, Complementary and Alternative Medicine." *Annals of Family Medicine*, vol. 7, no. 2, 2009, 139–147.

Young, Janine. "Clinical Pediatrics in the Mexican Immigrant Community." *Contemporary Pediatrics*, vol. 26, no. 4, 2009, 58–64.

Chapter 4

Giving directions to and at the hospital

LEARNING OUTCOMES FOR CHAPTER 4

Oral proficiency

Students will acquire the oral communicative skills that will allow them to appropriately interact in Spanish with their patients in the following ways:

- Provide information to patients and elicit information about location (floors and buildings) of places in the hospital.
- Provide and elicit directions.
- Provide and elicit addresses of health providers.
- Provide and elicit patient addresses.
- Describe and elicit descriptions of a patient's general physical condition.
- Describe and elicit descriptions of a patient's symptoms.
- Identify and elicit identifications of the parts of the body.
- Identify and elicit identifications of the organs in the body.

Cultural humility

Students will demonstrate an awareness of how to respond to patients with cultural humility when learning about the following Hispanic culturally based concepts or practices.
The Hispanic phenomena of *modestia* with respect to the body of a patient, in a clinical setting. They will take into consideration that this cultural concept is informed by the identity of the patient (age, gender and level of acculturation) as well as that of the accompanying family members. Always inquire about their personal preference with regard to the gender of the attending health professional or medical staff member.

A. Locations in the hospital and the verb (estar)

I. The verb (estar)

Yo estoy en	*Nosotros estamos en*
Tú estás en	
Ud, él, ella está en	*Uds, ellos, ellas están en*
Estoy en mi hospital	*Estoy en la planta baja*
Está en el consultorio	*Está en el primer piso*
Están en la entrada	*Están en el tercer piso*

 ¡OJO!

Note that when using the cardinal numbers with a masculine noun (here: *piso* "floor"), you drop the *o* for primer and tercer (*primer piso, segundo piso, tercer piso, cuarto piso, quinto piso, sexto piso*). The first floor or "ground floor" is the *planta baja*, the second floor is the *primer piso*, etc.

 Audio I *el verbo (estar) y la preposición en*

2. Questions with ¿dónde? and ¿en qué?

Use the information question word *¿dónde?* "where" when inquiring about general location. If you want to specifically ask "on what floor" or "in what building" a department or unit is located, use *¿En qué?*

¿Dónde está la paciente?	*La paciente está en el edificio principal.*
¿Dónde está su hospital?	*Mi hospital está en Akron.*
¿En qué edificio está el salón de clase?	*Está en Considere.*
¿En qué piso está la cafetería?	*La cafetería está en la planta baja ("ground floor").*

3. The preposición en and locación

Always use the preposition *en* ("in/at") with the verb *estar* when talking about location. See the conversation below.

Conversaciones breves

A. A young patient asks a doctor that she encounters in the hallway for the floor location of the waiting room.

—Perdón, doctor. ¿Dónde está la sala de espera? —La sala de espera está en el primer piso.
—Muchas gracias, doctor.
—De nada, señorita

B. A lost 30-year-old patient asks a doctor where she is.

—Perdón, doctor. ¿Dónde estoy?
—Señorita, usted está en el segundo piso del edificio principal de este hospital.
—Ah, muchas gracias, doctor.
—De nada, señorita.

Práctica escrita 1

Completar las oraciones con la forma correcta de *(estar):*

1. Los servicios _____ cerca de las escaleras.
2. La cafetería _____ al fondo del pasillo.
3. Usted _____ en la sala de recuperación.
4. Su madre _____ en la sala de espera.
5. Su bebé _____ con ("with") la enfermera.
6. El médico _____ en su consultorio.
7. Tú _____ en la tienda de regalos.
8. Nosotros _____ en la oficina administrativa.
9. Mis hermanos _____ en la recepción.
10. ¿Dónde _____ las enfermeras?
11. Su abuelo _____ en el centro de terapia física.
12. Nosotros _____ en la unidad de quemados.
13. Su familia _____ en la capilla.

Práctica escrita 2

Escribir 4 diálogos en español. Using the elements given, create a brief dialogue. Make sure you conjugate *(estar)* and make all of the adjustments and sentence order changes that you need. Note that you are both asking and answering questions in this activity.

1. ¿Doctor/estar/mi hijo?
   Estar/sala de recuperación/2.° piso

2. ¿Señorita/estar/sala de radiografías?
   Estar/4.° piso
3. ¿Señor/edificio/estar/yo?
   Estar/usted/Locust
4. ¿Enfermera/estar/los ascensores?
   Estar/1.er piso.
5. Señor/estar/capilla?
   Estar/ 3.er piso.

Práctica escrita 3

*Escribir **dónde** están.*

1. Tú/oficina administrativa.
2. Ellos/ departamento de cardiología.
3. Yo/unidad de cuidado neonatal.
4. Esposo/estacionamiento.
5. El taxi/entrada principal.
6. Familia/quiosco.

Práctica escrita 4

*Escribir **en qué pisos** están los pacientes o los empleados del hospital:*

1. Ellos/ 1.er piso.
2. La niña/4.° piso.
3. La familia/5.° piso.
4. La pediatra/3.er piso.
5. Los enfermeros/PB (ground floor).

Práctica escrita 5

Looking for places in the hospital. *¿En qué piso está? Usar esta información para después contestar las preguntas 1–5.*

La planta baja	servicios, sala de espera, tienda de regalos
1.er piso	recepción, entrada principal, laboratorios
2.° piso	unidad de cuidados críticos, sala de emergencias
3.er	estación de enfermeras, centro de cardiología
4.°	restaurantes, patología, servicios, capilla
5.°	cirugía, consultorios, oficinas administrativas, farmacia

1. La estación de enfermeras.
2. La unidad de cuidados críticos.

3. Los restaurantes.
4. La farmacia.
5. La sala de espera y la tienda de regalos.

Práctica escrita 6

Los pisos en el edificio de tu hospital. You have decided to make a guide of your building at your hospital. Using the guide/map in *práctica 5*, above, make your own guide indicating what places are on each floor. Use the vocabulary that we have learned.

Role-play 1

Inventar y escribir dos diálogos separados para esta interacción:
Paciente de 53 años / enfermera
Patient:

> Greet a nurse.
> Excuse yourself. (*Perdón* or *disculpe señorita / doctor*)
> Ask for your location.
> Ask for the location of a department or unit.
> Thank the nurse.
> Say goodbye.

Role-play 2

Inventar y escribir las dos partes de esta interacción: (Usted es el paciente)

> Stop doctor Salas and greet him.
> Ask him for the location of your child.
> Ask for the location of the recovery room.
> Thank him.
> Say goodbye.

Role-play 3

En el hospital. You are a receptionist and early one morning a 35-year-old woman walks into the waiting room with her young child. (*Remember to always use the Ud. form when addressing a patient, unless it is a child or a friend, and to always thank the patient for their assistance with a cordial: *¡Muchas gracias!* or to thank them in return, after having been thanked by them, using *¡Gracias a usted*!):

> She greets you.
> You ask her name and her child's name.
> She asks if she is in the waiting room of the pediatrician.
> You respond that it is the waiting room of another specialist (pick one).

She asks if the waiting room is in this building.
You respond that is in another building (provide one).
She asks if there are bathrooms on the first floor.
You respond negatively and provide a floor.
She thanks you and you close.

Práctica escrita 7

Crear dos nuevos diálogos para practicar en clase.

B. Giving directions

I. Adverbial expressions

For questions about specific location of places in the hospital, use
the following adverbial expressions and the verb (*estar*):

Al fondo de	(at the end of)
Al lado de / a la derecha de / a la izquierda de	(next to, to the right, to the left of)
Antes de / después de	(before / after)
Cerca de / lejos de	(close to / far from)
Enfrente de / delante de / detrás de	(facing, in front of, behind)
Entre	(between)

2. The preposition de

Note that all of these adverbial expressions are followed by *de* except
for *entre*

> *¿Dónde está el lavabo? El lavabo está cerca de las escaleras. El
> lavabo está entre el ascensor y las escaleras.*

3. Contractions de + el (del)

When using an adverbial expression with *de*, you will need to make a
contraction if the place that follows is masculine: *de + el = del*

> *del salón de clases, del puente, del piso, del estacionamiento, del
> banco de sangre, del pasillo, del edificio, del lavabo, del ascensor,
> etc.*

Contrast: *El lavabo está cerca del ascensor (de + el ascensor), cerca de
las escaleras, cerca de las oficinas, cerca de los consultorios.*

Audio 2 (expressions of location)

Práctica escrita 8

You will draw a brief sketch of the department or unit where you work to describe to a partner during class. Use the descriptions above to describe other units or places (next to you, across from you, etc.). Draw or create your sketch, but do not write the description. Just practice orally in order to be prepared for class.

Modelo: *Mi oficina está a la derecha de la cafetería, delante de los servicios y entre la sala de espera y otra oficina.*

Práctica escrita 9

En un edificio de mi hospital. Descripciones. Use the adverbial expressions you just learned to describe where these places are located, with respect to one another, in a particular building at your hospital or healthcare facility.

Modelo: En mi hospital, en el edificio X, la entrada está cerca de la recepción). Do not repeat expressions:

1. ¿Dónde está la entrada principal en relación a la recepción?
2. ¿Dónde están los servicios en relación a las escaleras?
3. ¿Dónde está la cafetería en relación a la tienda de regalos y la farmacia?
4. ¿Dónde está la capilla en relación a la farmacia?
5. ¿Dónde está la salida?
6. ¿Dónde está la salida en relación a la entrada principal?

C. Addresses, healthcare providers and patients

1. Addresses

When giving out addresses you are in fact identifying them. Use the verb (*ser*) to request and provide addresses. Use *plaza* for "square," *avenida* for "avenue," and *calle* for all others.

> *¿Cuál es la dirección del hospital Akron Children's? La dirección del hospital es plaza perkins 1, Akron, Ohio 44308* (4-4-3-0-8)
> *¿Cuál es su dirección, señorita? Mi dirección es calle Main 4381 (43–81) Akron 44302* (4-4-3-0-2)

2. Proper names

Do not translate the name of a street, city or state. Proper names are not translated.

3. ¿Qué? vs ¿Cuál?

Never use *¿qué?* in a question followed by the verb (*ser*) unless requesting a definition. Use *¿Cuál / es?*

¿Qué es un edificio?   ¿Cuál es el edificio cerca del estacionamiento?

Audio 3 (addresses) *direcciones*

Práctica oral I

Escribir los nombres de cuatro estudiantes en la clase de español. Preguntar la dirección y completar el diagrama.

E1. *¿Cuál es tu dirección?*

E2. *Mi dirección es calle Main 1122 (once-veintidós) Akron, Ohio, 44313 (4-4-3-1-3)*

Nombre	Calle	Número	Ciudad	Estado

Práctica escrita I0

¿Cuál es la dirección? Escribir la dirección de estos centros, edificios, hospitales y clínicas en español:

1. *ACH Heart Center:* 215 West Bowery Street, Suite 5200, Akron, Ohio 44308
2. *Summa Health Akron:* 525 East Market Street, Akron, Ohio 44304
3. *Akron General Hospital:* 400 Wabash Avenue, Akron, Ohio 44303
4. The *Crile Building* in the *Cleveland Clinic:* 2049 East 100th Street, Cleveland, Ohio 44195
5. *Dover Professional Bldg.* 4859 Dover Road, North Olmstead, Ohio 44070
6. *Euclid Hospital* 18901 Lakeshore Blvd, Euclid, Ohio 44119
7. *Falls Family Practice* 1900, 23rd Street, Cuyahoga Falls, Ohio 44223

D. Numbers 100–1000

Cien, ciento uno, ciento dos...	100, 101, 102...
Doscientos	200
Trescientos	300
Cuatrocientos	400
*Quinientos	**500**
Seiscientos	600
*Setecientos	**700**
Ochocientos	800
*Novecientos	**900**
Mil	1000

 ¡OJO!

The conjunction *y* (and) is only used with numbers between the tens and the units in 16–99. It is not used in the hundreds or thousands:

> *Diez* **y** *seis, noventa* **y** *nueve, but doscientos* **x** *nueve and dos* **x** *mil* **x** *nueve.*

 Audio 4 los números de 100–1000

E. Identifying symptoms with (tener)

1. General condition and the verb (estar)

When inquiring about general condition use the verb (*estar*) *¿Cómo está usted? Estoy bien, regular o así, así, mal, fatal, adolorido/a* (in pain) *decaído/a o deprimido/a* (downcast or depressed), *enfermo/a, mareado/a* (dizzy) *resfriado/a* (with flu-like symptoms) *mejor* (better), *peor* (worse).

2. Symptoms and the verb (tener)

Use *tener* + noun to describe symptoms or more specific conditions. Do not use a definite article with the symptoms in the list below except for "*los*" *ojos llorosos / rojos.*

> *¿Qué problema tiene usted hoy? Tengo congestión y tengo los ojos llorosos.*

3. Vocabulary of physical symptoms

Asma	
Calor	
Congestión	
Diarrea	
Dificultad para hablar	slurred speech
Dolor de / en el-la + parte del cuerpo	pain or discomfort in a part of the body
Ebriedad / borrachera	intoxication
Escalofríos	shivers
Estornudos	sneezing
Fiebre	fever
Frío	cold
Gripe	the flu
Indigestión	
Intoxicación	food poisoning
Irritación en el-la + parte del cuerpo	
Los ojos llorosos	runny eyes
Los ojos rojos	bloodshot eyes
Mareo	dizziness
Migrañas	
Mucosidad / mocos	
Náuseas	
Palpitaciones	
Picazón	itchiness
Ronchas	hives or raised rash
Sed	thirsty
Hambre	hungry
Temblores	
Sarpullido	rash
Tos	cough
Un resfrío / resfriado	a cold
Vértigo	
Vómitos	

4. Vocabulary of emotional symptoms

Tengo:	
Ansiedad	
Depresión	
Estrés en mi trabajo, familia, vida en general	
Insomnio	
Nervios	
Paranoia	
Pena	sadness

¡OJO!

Intoxicación is a false cognate. It does not mean "intoxicated," but rather "suffering from food poisoning." Always make sure that you understand the usage of ambiguous terms that may appear to be cognates by your patient. Depending on the level of acculturation to the US the patient may or may not be using it as true cognate. Misinterpretations can have serious consequences in a medical setting. If your interpreter cannot ask for a clarification, ask back-up questions to make sure that you understand exactly what is being said.

 Audio 5 los síntomas físicos y emocionales

 Práctica escrita 11

¿Cómo está y qué problema tiene mi paciente? Escribir los síntomas usando frases completas y el verbo (tener). In most cases, there is more than 1 choice for each image. Write all of the possibilities:

Modelo: *El está fatal. Tiene*....

1._____

2._____

3._____

4._____

5._____

6._____

7._____

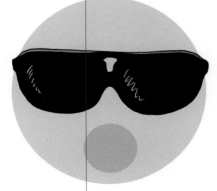

8._____

9._____

10._____

11._____

F. Identifying parts of the body and organs in the body

1. Vocabulary of the parts of the body

FEMENINO

La cabeza	the head
La cara	the face
La frente	the forehead
La boca	the mouth
La barbilla	the chin
La lengua	the tongue
La nariz	the nose
La oreja	the ear
La garganta	the throat
La mano	the hand
La mano derecha o izquierda	
La muñeca	the wrist
La espalda	the back
Las costillas	the ribs
La barriga	the belly
La cadera	the hip
La pierna	the leg
La rodilla	the knee (or the entire leg for some Mexican American Spanish-speakers)
La espinilla	the shin
La pantorrilla	the calf

MASCULINO

Los ojos	the eyes
Los labios	the lips
Los oídos	inside of ear
El cuello	the neck
El hombro	the shoulder
El brazo	the arm
El brazo derecho	right arm
El brazo izquierdo	left arm
El codo	the elbow
El dedo	the finger
El pecho	the chest
El ombligo	the belly button
El abdomen	the abdomen
Los glúteos	the buttocks
El tobillo	the ankle
El pie	the foot
Los dedos del pie	the toes
El talón	the heel

2. Vocabulary of the organs in the body

FEMENINOS

La vesícula	the gall bladder

MASCULINOS

El corazón	the heart
El estómago	the stomach
Los pulmones	the lungs
El hígado	the liver
El páncreas	the pancreas
Los riñones	the kidneys
Los intestinos	the intestines

3. Use of the definite article with the body

Use the definite article with the body, not the possessive adjective. This vocabulary section is deliberately organized in masculine and feminine columns, so that you pay special attention to the gender of the body parts or organs.

Audio 6 (part of the body and organs) *las partes del cuerpo y los órganos*

Cultura I *(modestia* and the body)

Modestia is related to *respeto* and should be recognized in a medical setting. Although the degree of *modestia* may vary with the Hispanic patient's identity and level of acculturation, a conversation about cultural practices and personal comfort with regard to physical exposure should take place before examining a Hispanic patient. Generally, when conducting a physical examination, it is recommended to use a robe (*una bata*) or a sheet (*una sábana*) to cover bodies prior to and during a physical examination and expose only the area of the body that is going to be examined (Chong, 2002). Sometimes the presence of a chaperone, if a same-sex physician is not available, can alleviate the uneasiness of the patient. With respect to sexual issues, a female patient may be more willing to disclose information with a female physician (Julliard et al., 2008).

Source: www.aafp.org/afp/2013/0101/p48.html

Audio 7 (parts of the body)

Partes del cuerpo. Listen to the paragraph in Audio 7. You will hear a series of body parts. As you hear each, circle and number the body part in the correct order:

El juego de tenis

_____ tobillo	_____ pie
_____ nariz	_____ dedo
_____ mano	_____ garganta
_____ boca	_____ cuello
_____ ojos	_____ muñeca
_____ brazos	_____ espalda
_____ barbilla	_____ orejas
_____ rodillas	_____ piernas
_____ pecho	

Práctica escrita 12

Escribir la parte correcta del cuerpo para los números 1–26. Usar izquierdo/izquierda o derecho/derecha cuando sea apropiado:

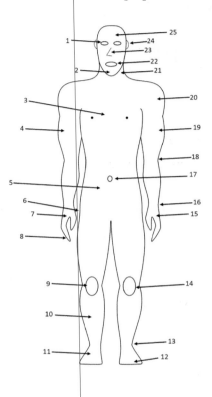

Práctica escrita 13

Los síntomas. Read the following descriptions and say what possible part or parts of the body would hurt this patient. Remember that if using *dolor de*, no definite article is needed before the body part or organ. However, if you chose *dolor en el/la/los/las*, you will have to pay special attention to the gender of the body part or organ.

1. She sits in school in an uncomfortable chair for hours: *Ella tiene dolor....*
2. A little boy sprained his ankle:
3. A child has a runny nose and has been blowing his nose constantly:
4. A teenager was long boarding and had a hard fall:
5. She has allergies:
6. María has been throwing up all night:

7. Pablo needs glasses and has been straining his eyes in school:
8. A boy has asthma:
9. A patient's son was injured playing soccer:

Práctica oral 2

Pair work: Your classmate is an elderly patient with the flu:

Ask for general condition with (*estar*).
Ask for symptoms (*tener*).
Ask if the body parts of the patient that are relevant to the symptom presented hurt him/her.
Ask about other body parts or organs.
¿Tiene dolor de / en el / la / los / las...?

After you have finished, switch roles.
Finally, be ready to report to the class:
Mi paciente está.... tiene dolor de (en el/la).... Mi paciente no tiene dolor de (en el/la).

Role-play 4

En el consultorio del pediatra. The 29-year-old mother of a 7-year-old girl has just arrived at the hospital. Neither of them speaks English. The child appears to be in a lot of pain:

Greet the mother.
Introduce yourself.
Ask the mother for her name.
Ask her for the name and age of the child.
Ask for the child's general condition.
Ask about her physical symptoms.
Ask about her emotional symptoms.
Ask if different body parts hurt.
Close the conversation.

Role-play 5

En la sala de emergencias. A 27-year-old man is brought into the Emergency Room. The friend that brings him in says he has *intoxicación*. Play the part of the ER nurse and try to determine if the young man is drunk or suffering from food poisoning by asking about the relevant symptoms.

Bibliography

Chong, Nilda. "CARE: Performing a Culturally Sensitive Patient Evaluation," *The Latino Patient*. Intercultural Press, 2002, pp. 141–169.

Hollingshead, Nicole A. et al. "The Pain Experience of Hispanic Americans: A Critical Literature Review and Conceptual Model." *The Journal of Pain: Official Journal of the American Pain Society*, vol. 17, no. 5, 2016, 513–528.

Juckett, Gregory. "Caring for Latino Patients." *American Family Physician*, vol. 87, no. 1, 2013, 48–54.

Julliard, Kell et al. "What Latina Patients Don't Tell Their Doctors: A Qualitative Study." *Annals of Family Medicine*, vol. 6, no. 6, 2008, 543–549.

Making appointments and describing weekly schedules

LEARNING OUTCOMES FOR CHAPTER 5

Oral proficiency

Students will acquire the oral communicative skills that will allow them to appropriately interact in Spanish with their patients in the following ways:

- Discuss time.
- Discuss at what time an event takes place.
- Make appointments with patients using the days of the week and the time.
- Negotiate scheduling complications successfully and make the appointment.
- Talk about their own availability during the week.
- Identify and talk about weekly schedules and activities of patients.
- Use the present tense to talk about daily and weekly activities and those of their patients or colleagues.
- Describe in the present tense.
- Narrate in the present tense using ar verbs and transition words of chronology.

Cultural humility

Students will demonstrate an awareness of how to respond to patients with cultural humility when learning about the following Hispanic culturally based concepts or practices:

- The fluidity of the Hispanic notion of time.
- Expectations of punctuality when making medical appointments.

A. The days of the week

1. Vocabulary of the days of the week

lunes	Monday
martes	Tuesday
miércoles	Wednesday
jueves	Thursday
viernes	Friday
sábado(s)	Saturday
domingo(s)	Sunday

2. Gender and number of the days of the week

The days of the week are all masculine. Since they already end in an "s," they do not change in the plural form, except for sábado(s) and domingo(s) that end in vowels.

3. Capitalization

The days of the week are never capitalized in Spanish.

4. The demonstrative adjective

The demonstrative adjective "this" is *este / esta / estos / estas*. It precedes the noun it describes:

> *Este lunes estoy en el hospital. Esta semana tengo vacaciones.*

 ¡OJO!

Never use the preposition *en* in Spanish when saying "on," as in "on Monday," "on Tuesday," etc. Use the definite article instead.

"**On** Tuesday": *El martes.* "**On** Tuesdays": *Los martes.*

 Audio 1 *los días de la semana*

 Práctica escrita 1

Estudiar de memoria los días de la semana. Now test your memory by writing both the day that precedes and the day that follows the day of the week provided below:

1. lunes:
2. viernes:

3. sábado:
4. jueves:
5. martes:
6. domingo:
7. miércoles:

 Práctica escrita 2

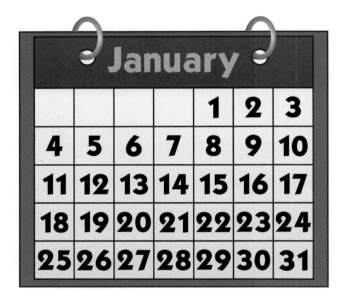

El calendario. Identificación de los días de la semana. Responder con frases completas:

1. ¿Cuántos lunes hay en enero?
2. ¿Qué día de la semana es el 18 de enero?
3. ¿Qué día de la semana es el primero de enero?
4. ¿Qué día es el siete de enero?
5. ¿Qué día es el quince?
6. ¿Qué día es el nueve?
7. ¿Qué día es el primero?
8. ¿Cuántos sábados hay en enero?
9. ¿Hay cinco viernes en enero?
10. ¿Qué días son el cinco y el veintisiete?
11. ¿Qué días son el veintiuno y el veintidós?

Práctica escrita 3

Los días de la semana. Responder con frases completas.

1. ¿Tienes pacientes los viernes?
2. ¿Qué días no tienes pacientes?
3. ¿Qué días estás en el hospital?
4. ¿Qué días estás en tu casa?
5. ¿Cuántos días por (per) semana estás en el hospital?
6. ¿Cuál es el primer día de la semana en los Estados Unidos?
7. ¿Cuál es el primer día de la semana para los hispanos?
8. ¿Tienen ustedes pacientes todos los días?
9. ¿Está usted en el hospital los fines de semana?

*Go back and re-read the first and last questions. Notice that there is no *en* before the days of the week or weekend, but rather a *los* to indicate "on." Now re-read your answers. Did you mistakenly add *en* to your answers?

Práctica escrita 4

Mi horario en el hospital. Look at the calendar for next month. Use 2 sentences for each number. First, **identify** the day of the week using the correct form of "ser." Then, say whether you **are at** the hospital on that day of the week, using the correct form of "estar" [Remember that "in/at" in Spanish is *en*. <u>Never</u> use "en" with the days of the week. Do use the preposition *en* with the verb (*estar*) when talking about location]:

    Modelo: el tres: El tres es martes. No estoy en el hospital los martes.

1. el dos:
2. el veintinueve:
3. el quince:
4. el veintiocho:
5. el siete:
6. el dieciséis:
7. el diez:
8. el once:
9. el veintisiete:
10. el primero:

Práctica escrita 5

La sala de emergencias. You and a colleague are working on your schedule in the ER next month. You have decided to take the MWF shift and your colleague prefers the TTh schedule. Using a current calendar:

Write down the days and dates that you are in the ER on week 3.

Write down the days you are not there on week 1.

Write the days your colleague is in the ER on week 2. This will require you asking him for that schedule. (*¿En la segunda semana, qué días estás...?*)

Use full sentences:

1. En la tercera semana:
2. En la primera semana:
3. En la segunda semana:

Práctica oral I

El consultorio del médico. You and a fellow assistant are comparing the days you work this month, because you would like to get together. Discuss the days you work and the days that you are free each week using full sentences.

Role-play I

Su hija tiene una cita. You are a receptionist in a pediatrician's office. The 33-year-old mother of a new patient calls on the phone for information about an appointment that has already been made for her daughter in July. (Make sure that you vary the content of this role-play with every partner and that you always thank your patient for her collaboration: *¡Muchas gracias, señora!* or *¡gracias a usted!*)

Greet her appropriately taking into consideration her marital status.
Introduce yourself (make up fictitious names for you and the doctor).
Ask for the mother's full name.
Ask 4 relevant questions about the child (personal and medical).
Remind her that she has an appointment with the doctor.
The patient asks for building and floor location of pediatrician's office.
Respond appropriately.
Patient confirms location of office by asking if it is "close to" department (provide choice).
Respond affirmatively or negatively. (If negatively, provide further descriptions of hospital places so that she can orient herself.)
Patient asks for the date of the appointment.
Provide a date.
Patient asks for day of the week.
Provide day of the week.
Thank the provider for her help.
Close.

B. Telling time

1. Time and the verb (ser) *¿Qué hora es?*

Telling time is in fact "identifying" the time of the day. The verb (*ser*) is the verb used to identify in Spanish. When talking about the time, use the verb (*ser*) along with the feminine definite article, *la(s)* since *hora* is feminine. However, note that *hora* is only used in the questions. Never in the answer.

> *¿Qué hora es?*
>
> *Es la una*
> *Es mediodía*   *en punto* ("on the dot")
> *Es medianoche*

2. Number (es vs son)

When identifying the time with a plural number (2:00, 3:00, 4:00, etc.), you must use the plural form of (*ser*): *son* along with the plural definite article: *las.*

> *¿Qué hora es?*
>
> *Son las dos, las tres, las cuatro, las cinco, las seis, las siete, las ocho, las nueve, las diez, las once, las doce.*

Audio 2 la hora y el verbo (ser)

Práctica escrita 6

La hora. Escribir el verbo en la forma correcta para identificar la hora:
¿es or son?

1. Medianoche
2. Las dos:
3. La una:
4. Las tres:
5. Las nueve:
6. Mediodía:
7. Las doce:
8. Las cuatro:

9. Las diez:
10. Las once:

 Práctica escrita 7

¿Qué hora es? Responder con frases completas y con la expresión en punto "on the dot":

1. 3:00
2. 1:00
3. 9:00
4. 7:00
5. 12 pm
6. 12 am

---

3. Before and after the time (menos and y)

When not saying *en punto*, use *y* to state minutes "after" the hour (minutes between 1 and 30). Use *menos* to state minutes "before" the next hour (minutes between 31 and 59).

4. Am and pm

Use *de + la mañana, de la tarde y de la noche* when telling time.

De la mañana	*Son las nueve de la mañana.*
De la tarde	*Es la una de la tarde.*
De la noche	*Son las diez de la noche.*

5. Saying 15 minutes before or after the hour.

The expression *cuarto* "quarter" is used as well as *quince* for 15 minutes:

5:15 *Son las cinco y cuarto* (or *son las cinco y quince*). 5:45 *Son las seis menos cuarto* (or *son las seis menos quince*)

6. Saying half past the hour

The expression *y media is* used, as well as *y treinta*, for "half past" the hour.

Son las cinco y media (or *son las cinco y treinta*).

7. Clocks and watches

There is only one word in Spanish for both clocks and watches: *el reloj*. Context distinguishes one from the other.

Audio 3 la hora

Práctica escrita 8

La hora. ¿Qué hora es? Escribir la hora completa (no digits):

1. 3:15 pm
2. 1:25 pm
3. 11:05 am
4. 9:10 pm
5. 7:45 am
6. 8:50 pm
7. 12:00 pm
8. 12:56 am
9. 6:43 am
10. 6:17 pm

Práctica oral 2 (en clase)

Identificación de la hora correcta. ¿Qué hora es la correcta? Escuchar a la profesora y dibujar "draw" *la hora en los relojes.* (Listen and draw the correct time on the face.)

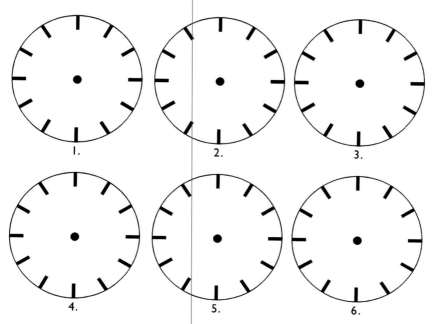

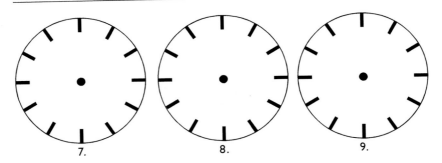

7.   8.   9.

 Práctica escrita 9

¿Qué hora es? Escribir la hora correcta (todas las posibilidades) para cada reloj.

1.

2.

3.

4.

 Cultura 1 **(punctuality)**

The concept of time and expectations of punctuality may differ between a Hispanic and a non-Hispanic patient. Some patients may consider that responsibilities to family take precedence over other obligations, including medical appointments. As a result of their cultural priorities, they may not even explain or apologize for a no-show because they assume that the medical staff shares these cultural priorities practices. Healthcare staff or practitioners should take the time to discuss practices and expectations of punctuality when making appointments with their patients.

Práctica oral 3 (en clase)

El horario de los empleados. Work schedules. (1) Respond to a variety of questions asked by the instructor by looking at this chart. (2) Now work in pairs and ask each other questions:

Nombre completo	profesión	lugar de trabajo	días libres (free days)
Isabel Truyols Orozco	pediatra	Consultorio	LM
Alicia Aguilar Roselló	terapeuta	Centro de terapia física	J
José Rullán Vicéns	enfermero	Sala de emergencias	S y D
Carlos Martínez Vives	cirujano	Departamento de ortopedia	M J
Paz Buades Rivas	directora	Unidad de cuidados	L
Concha Roca Tous	cardióloga	Centro del corazón	VS

Role-play 2

¿Qué hora es? A 55-year-old patient is walking down the corridors of the hospital looking for a clock. She stops a hospital employee to ask questions. Dramatize this encounter. Make sure that you vary the content of this role-play with every partner:

> Greet the employee.
> Ask for the time.
> Thank him/her.
> Employee asks you if you have an appointment (*una cita*).
> Answer affirmatively saying in what department, unit or center you have the appointment and then ask for its location.
> Employee answers with information about building, floor and one descriptor (adverbial expression).
> Close.

---

8. ¿A qué hora?

Generally, the preposition *en* is used in Spanish with the verb "estar" when talking about location and to say "in" or "at." (*Estoy en el hospital los lunes*). However, when asking "at what time" an activity occurs, *a* is used to mean "at." You will also use *a* in your answer.

> *¿A qué hora está usted en el hospital por la mañana? Estoy en el hospital a las 7:30 de la mañana.*

When asking this question, you are not required to use the verb (*ser*) since you are not identifying (telling or asking) time. You are inquiring at what time an activity occurs. Notice the use of *a* to mean "at" when telling time in the question and answer.

Contrast these 2 questions below:

¿Qué horas es? (Here you are identifying or telling time). *Son las ocho de la mañana.*
¿A qué horas está en el hospital? (Here you are not telling time, you are referring to when an activity or event occurs). *Estoy en el hospital a las ocho de la mañana.*

9. ¿Cuándo?

A more general question is asked using the interrogative word: *¿Cuándo?* "When?"

¿Cuándo está en el hospital los lunes? This question can be answered with a specific time in the answer *(a las + hora)* or with a more general *por la mañana* "in the morning".

10. **De** la mañana / **por** la mañana

When referring specifically to clock time, use *de* + (*la mañana, la tarde, la noche*):

*Estoy en el hospital <u>a las ocho</u> <u>**de**</u> la mañana.*

When referring more broadly to time, that is without any specific clock reference, use *por* (*la mañana, la tarde, la noche*)

*Estoy en el hospital **por** la mañana.*

11. Adverbs of habit

Generalmente "generally" and *usualmente* "usually" are used with the present tense to express habit.

12. Availability

When asking or reporting on "availability" or "free time" use the expression *"estar libre"*: *Los lunes usualmente **estoy libre** a las once de la mañana.*

 ### *Conversación breve*

—Perdón (o"disculpe") señor, ¿qué hora es?
—Son las diez de la mañana, señorita.
—¿Estoy en el edificio principal de este hospital?
—No señorita. El edificio principal está en otra calle. ¿A qué hora es su cita?
—Mi cita es a las diez en punto en el primer piso del edificio principal.

Práctica escrita 10

¿A qué hora? Responder con frases completas:

1. ¿A qué hora tienes clase de español los lunes por la tarde?
2. ¿A qué hora estás en el estacionamiento del hospital los martes por la mañana?
3. ¿A qué hora estás en la cafetería del hospital usualmente?
4. ¿A qué hora estás en tu oficina generalmente por la mañana?
5. ¿A qué hora estás en tu casa después (after) de la clase de español?
6. ¿A qué horas estás libre usualmente los jueves?

C. Talking about daily activities. The present tense of -ar verbs

1. Present tense of regular -ar verbs

-ar verbs end in an "-ar" in the infinitive form. (The infinitive is the non-personalized form or name of the verb and is often written in a parenthesis):

(*Trabajar*): to work

Regular -ar verbs are all conjugated using the same pattern and the same set of endings. To conjugate a regular -ar verb in the present tense, remove the *ar* off the infinitive and add the personalized endings: *o, as, a, amos, an*:

(*Trabajar*):	
Yo trabaj **o**	*nosotros / as trabaj* **amos**
Tú trabaj **as**	
Ud/él/ella trabaj **a**	*Uds/ellos/ellas trabaj* **an**

 Audio 4 el presente de los verbos -ar

 Práctica escrita 11

Identificar los verbos -ar de esta lista de infintivos. Circle only the regular -ar verbs from this list of infinitives:

1. (ser), 2. (trabajar), 3. (haber), 4. (Llamarse), 5. (estar), 6. (comer), 7. (tener), 8. (ver), 9. (hablar), 10. (asistir), 11. (necesitar), 12. (vivir), 13. (querer), 14. (invitar), 15. (escribir), 16. (escuchar), 17. (revisar)

Práctica escrita 12

El verbo (trabajar). Completar con la forma correcta del verbo.

1. Yo _____ en la Universidad de Akron.
2. Ella _____ en su oficina.
3. ¿Dónde _____ tú?
4. Nosotros_____ en el consultorio.
5. Tú _____ en la sala de operaciones.
6. El pediatra_____con los niños.
7. Ustedes _____en la farmacia.
8. Ellos _____ en la tienda de regalos.
9. El médico _____ en la sala de emergencias.
10. El aparcacoches_____en la entrada del hospital y en el estacionamiento.

2. Vocabulary. Additional regular -ar verbs

Levantarse: to get up in the morning

Ducharse / lavarse: to shower / wash
Desayunar: to have breakfast
Manejar: to drive
Aparcar en: to park

Llegar a to arrive
Caminar a: to walk

Hablar / conversar / charlar
Celebrar
Comprar: to buy
Escuchar a

Entrar en

Estudiar
Preguntar: to ask
Contestar el teléfono: to answer
Apuntar: to take notes

*With reflexive verbs like (*llamarse*) use *me, te se, nos* and *se* before the verb.

(*su carro*)
(*el garaje, el estacionamiento del hospital o la calle*)
(*la cita*)
(*la sala de espera, al departamento / la unidad / el centro de*)
(*con su paciente o colega*)

(*comida en la cafetería*)
(*su médico, la recepcionista o la enfermera*)
(*el hospital / la clínica, el consultorio,* etc.)

(*a la profesora o a sus colegas*)

(*información médica, preguntas para el médico o la enfermera*)

Necesitar: to need
Mirar: to look at
Buscar: to look for

(*ayuda*: help or *atención médica*)
(*televisión*)
(*un lugar en el hospital* o
*información médica en el
internet*)

Tomar medicina
Preparar el almuerzo: lunch
Visitar
Terminar: to finish
Regresar: to return
Cenar: to have your dinner

(*o una merienda*: "snack")
(*a su médico, otro hospital*)
(*el antibiótico*)
(*a su casa*)
(*comida saludable*)

Reflexive verbs (levantarse and ducharse) (*Levantarse*) and (*ducharse*)
have a reflexive pronoun *se* after the infinitive -ar ending. Just like
(*llamarse*). You must place the reflexive pronouns *me, te, se,* or *nos*
before your conjugated verb: *Yo **me** levanto.*

3. The verb "to do" (hacer)

What do you do? *¿Qué hace usted? ¿Qué haces tú?* Use the verb
(*hacer*) in order to ask about a patient's or colleague's habits. Only
use it in the question. In the answer use the appropriate verb(s) that
describes the activity:

*¿Generalmente qué **hace** usted los lunes a las 7:45 de la mañana?*
*Generalmente yo **aparco** mi carro a las 7:45 de la mañana.*

Práctica escrita 13

Contestar las preguntas con frases completes. ¡No usar el verbo *hacer*! Usar
un verbo regular ar de la lista en (C.2).
   En su casa: ¿Qué hace usted por la mañana los lunes?

1.
2.
3.

En el hospital: ¿Qué hace usted por la tarde?

1.
2.
3.
4.

En su casa: ¿Qué hace usted por la noche?

1.
2.
3.

Práctica oral 4 (en clase)

Hablar a sus colegas de sus actividades diarias. Usar días diferentes en sus preguntas, "por" sin la hora, y "de" con la hora.

   Modelo: ¿Qué haces los lunes por la mañana, usualmente? Los lunes por la mañana yo me levanto y desayuno. ¿Qué haces a las nueve de la mañana?

Día	Nombre	Actividad en el presente
Los lunes por la mañana	**María**	**Ella se levanta y desayuna**
Los martes por la noche		
Los miércoles al mediodía		
Los jueves a las diez de la mañana		
Los viernes a las tres de la tarde		
Los sábados por la mañana		
Los domingos por la tarde		

Práctica escrita 14

¿A qué hora? La doctora Pérez Ruíz trabaja mucho hoy. Mirar su agenda y decir o escribir a qué hora tiene estas actividades:

AGENDA DE LA DRA:

1. 6:45 Buscar estacionamiento.
2. 6:50 Aparcar en la calle.
3. 7:00 Entrar en el hospital.
4. 8:00 Desayunar con colegas.
5. 9:30 Visitar a los pacientes en el departamento de cardiología.
6. 11:00 Cita en el consultorio con la señora Payas Gil.
7. 12:00 Restaurante Las Margaritas con su esposo.
8. 1:15 Hablar por teléfono con el Dr. López.
9. 1:30 El café Starbucks.
10. 2:25 Consultorio con nuevos pacientes.
11. 3:30 Navegar el internet.
12. 3:45 Tomar una merienda en el consultorio.
13. 4:00 Terminar el trabajo del día.
14. 5:30 Charlar con sus colegas en una reunión importante.

15. 8:00 Reservaciones en el restaurante italiano.
16. 9:30 En casa.

¿A qué hora tiene ella estas actividades? Consultar la agenda de la doctora y completar con la hora correcta:

1. La doctora está en el consultorio con nuevos pacientes...
2. Ella charla con sus colegas en una reunión importante...
3. Ella aparca su coche en la calle enfrente del hospital...
4. Ella visita a sus pacientes en el departamento de cardiología...
5. Ella llega al hospital...
6. Ella mira su programa favorito en la tele con su familia...
7. Ella toma su almuerzo con su esposo...
8. La doctora desayuna con colegas en la cafetería del hospital...
9. Ella toma un café en Starbucks con la madre de un paciente...
10. Ella habla por teléfono con su colega el Dr. López...
11. Ella termina su trabajo...
12. Ella busca información en el internet...
13. Ella regresa a su casa...
14. Ella toma una merienda en su oficina...

 Práctica escrita 15

Las actividades diarias y los horarios. Responder con frases completas. (Notice that reflexive verbs are preceded by the reflexive pronoun *te* below. You must use a *me* in your answer):

1. ¿A qué hora te levantas los lunes por la mañana?
2. ¿A qué hora desayunas los lunes? ¿Y los domingos?
3. ¿Qué haces los martes a las tres de la tarde?
4. ¿Qué haces los viernes a las siete de la tarde?
5. ¿A qué hora estudias para nuestra clase?
6. ¿A qué hora llegas al hospital los jueves?
7. ¿A qué hora regresas a tu casa los viernes por la tarde?
8. ¿Qué haces los sábados a las once de la mañana?
9. ¿Dónde compras tus bebidas en el hospital?
10. ¿Te duchas por las mañanas o por las noches?

 Práctica escrita 16

Imagen de un empleada del hospital. Descripción. Create and write a story about this hospital employee in 2 parts. For this *práctica*, you will write the background description by using a) what <u>you see</u> in the image and b) <u>your imagination</u>. First, explain who/what appears (exists) in the image (*haber*).

Identify (*ser*) day, time. What are their names, ages? Identify *(ser)* profession. Describe (ser) physical characteristics and personality of both people in the image. Tell where they are located (*estar*). Use all of these verbs for your description: *(haber)*, *(ser)*, *(llamarse)*, *(tener)* and *(estar)*.

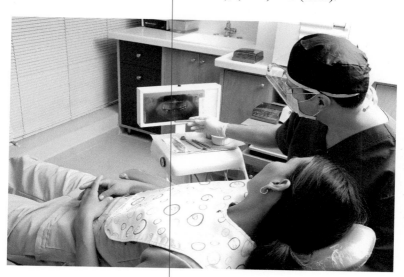

 ## Práctica escrita 17

Fotografía de una empleada del hospital. Narración. Look at the image of the nurse on page 94 and write a narration in the present tense. What does she do next? What does she do at her job in the hospital all day and later when she returns home? For the narration, use as many possible regular ar verbs and the following transition words to set up your chronology.

Primero	First
Después / luego	Then
Más tarde	Later
Por la mañana	In the morning
Por la tarde	In the afternoon
Por la noche	In the evening
A las...	At +time
Finalmente.	Finally
Al final del día	At the end of the day

 ## Práctica oral 5 (en casa)

Descripción y narración. Practice creating a couple of brief oral stories with different descriptions and narrations in the present tense based on what you see in the image. Use the structures and writing tips in prácticas 16 and 17

to aid you. Do not write sentences down for this activity. You may jot down a list of useful words or the list of infinitive that you are planning to use, but no phrases or sentences.

 ### Role-play 3

Una cita con el terapeuta. A 43-year-old patient discusses the next appointment with her therapist.

> Therapist asks what days the patient works next week (*la semana próxima*).
> Therapist asks if the patient is available or free on Friday.
> Patient responds that he or she is home with mom.
> Therapist asks what time the patient is free on another free day in the afternoon.
> Patient replies with a time.
> Therapist accepts and closes the conversation confirming with the patient the time/date of the appointment at his office.

 ### Role-play 4

Una cita con el paciente. The receptionist is making an appointment with a 52-year-old patient who has a very busy schedule. Pull out a calendar for this month on your cell or personal planner, so that you can work out the appointment date and time. Make sure that you vary the content of this role-play with every partner:

Ask the patient when (*cuándo*) or at what times (*a qué horas*) he is available or free on a particular day of the week and date, in the morning or afternoon.
Patient is not free.
Ask the patient if he is free another day, date and time.
He is not and provides an excuse. (Mentions a particular activity with an ar verb.)
Finally, you both decide on a morning (day of the week and date).
Close the conversation.

Chapter 6

Completing hospital forms and requesting patient information

LEARNING OUTCOMES FOR CHAPTER 6

Oral proficiency

Students will acquire the oral communicative skills that will allow them to appropriately interact in Spanish with their patients in the following ways:

- Elicit information using questions words *¿Qué?* and *¿Cuál?*
- Identify the months of the year.
- Create and talk about monthly schedules and holidays.
- Identify and state dates correctly.
- Schedule an appointment over the phone.
- Request and give birthdates.
- Take a patient's contact information.
- Take a patient's weight and height.
- Take information on marital status.
- Take information on nationality and identity documents.
- Take information on medical insurance and policy or group number.

Cultural humility

Students will demonstrate an awareness of how to respond to patients with cultural humility when learning about:

- Celebration of holidays observed and not observed in the US, by their Hispanic patients.
- The impact of high uninsured rates in Hispanic communities and their practices with regard to visits to primary care physicians.

A. Interrogative words. Information questions

I. What? ¿Qué vs Cuál / es? with the verb (ser)

Although both words mean "what?", the interrogative word *qué* is used exclusively with the verb (*ser*) when requesting a definition:

> *¿Qué es un cirujano? Un cirujano es un médico que opera a sus pacientes.*

In all other case *¿cuál(es)* is used. If the information requested is plural *cuáles* is used with the plural form of the verb (*ser*): *son*. See examples below:

2. Vocabulary. Interrogative questions with ¿Cuál(es)?

> *¿Cuál es su nombre?* (More appropriate on a form question than the more conversational question: *¿Cómo se llama usted?*)
> *¿Cuáles son sus apellidos?*
> *¿Cuál es su nombre completo? ¿el nombre completo de su madre? ¿de su padre?*
> *¿Cuál es su dirección? ¿Su dirección electrónica?*
> *¿Cuál es el número de su oficina? ¿de su teléfono fijo? ¿de su teléfono celular?*
> *¿Cuál es su edad?* (More appropriate on a form than the more conversational question¿*Cuántos años tiene usted*)
> *¿Cuál es su profesión?*

3. Written accent marks and interrogative words

All interrogative words are spelled with accent marks or tildes on the vowel that is stressed when pronouncing the word: *Cómo, Cuál(s)l, Cuándo, Dónde, En qué, Cuántos / as.*

Audio 1 *palabras interrogativas*

Práctica escrita 1

Palabras interrogativas. Leer estas respuestas y escribir las preguntas correspondientes con las palabras interrogativas apropiadas. Read the following responses and write the appropriate information question with the appropriate interrogative word:

1. Tengo 13 años:
2. Mi nombre es María.

3. Mi dirección en México es calle Son Españolet 36. Puebla, México.
4. Mi dirección en los Estados Unidos es calle Merriman 22, Akron, Ohio.
5. Mi dirección electrónica es marissa@ (arroba) uakron. (punto) edu.
6. Mis apellidos son Miralles Rivas.
7. Mi número de teléfono es 330 7012798.
8. El número de mi oficina es (216) 9810309, extensión 23.
9. No tengo teléfono fijo.
10. Soy cocinera.

 Práctica oral I (en clase)

Ask a classmate questions in order to obtain this information:
Full name.
Age.
Full name of parents.
Home address, work address and e-mail address.
Home, work and cell numbers.
Profession or occupation.
Be ready to share the patient information with the class.

B. Identifying the date

1. The date ¿Cuál es la fecha de hoy?

Use this structure to answer questions about the date:

			de + mil	
(Hoy) Es _____	*, el* _____	*de* _____	*del + 2 mil* _____	
day of week	date	month		year

Hoy es lunes, el 4 de agosto del 2020.

Es lunes
Es agosto
Es el 4

2. Use and omission of the definite article with the date

Do not use the definite article with the days of the week or with the months. Do use it before digits.

3. The month of the year

Los meses del año. The months (except for *enero*: January) are cognates and easy to recognize and identify. Like the days of the week, the months are not capitalized

> *enero*
> *febrero*
> *marzo*
> *abril*
> *mayo*
> *junio*
> *julio*
> *agosto*
> *se(p)tiembre*
> *octubre*
> *noviembre*
> *diciembre*

4. Abbreviating dates

In Spanish the abbreviation follows the same sequence as the full answer to the date: day/month/year:

> *El 4 de agosto del 2020* is abbreviated *4/08/2020* in Spanish. (Contrast this with the abbreviation in US English where the month precedes the day: 08/04/2020.)

 ¡OJO!

Months are mostly cognates; however, their similarity to English can lead to spelling errors. Note that the fall and early winter months that are cognates in English and end in "ember": "Sept**ember**," "Nov**ember**" and "Dec**ember**" end in *iembre* in Spanish: *se(p)tiembre, noviembre* y *diciembre*.

 Audio 2 los meses y las fechas

Cultura I (hispanic celebrations)

Hispanics may celebrate holidays that are not typically celebrated in the US, for example, *Día de Muertos/*The Day of the Dead. *Día de los Muertos* is a national, religious holiday in Mexico that is celebrated from October 31 to

November 2. It is a festive holiday that commemorates the death of loved ones with altars, flowers, favorite foods and parades. There is some evidence that this cultural practice can shape the relationships that some of the elderly hold with death and may be a reducer of death anxiety (Krause and Elena, 2012). Generally, religion and spirituality can help influence the experience of terminal illness. Healthcare provider exploration of the beliefs of their terminally ill patients and their family members can be valuable in supporting them through palliative care (Smith et al., 2009).

Source: www.cdc.gov/healthcommunication/pdf/audience/audienceinsight_cultural insights.pdf

Práctica escrita 2

¿Cuál es la fecha de hoy? Responder con frases completas:

1. 2/12/1982
2. 29/10/2004
3. 16/07/1996
4. 30/04/2011
5. 14/02/1954
6. 7/01/2018
7. 1/05/1976
8. 21/11/2009
9. 19/03/2000

Práctica escrita 3

El lugar de trabajo en el hospital y las celebraciones. As an employee in a pediatric hospital, you like to keep your workplace decorated for the children. Write the name in Spanish of the month or months when you would be likely to use the following decorations or themes:

1. Santa Claus.
2. Bunnies and Easter eggs.
3. Ghosts and witches.
4. Fireworks and flags.
5. Hearts and cupids.
6. Pumpkins.
7. Mother baking a pie.

8. Father throwing a football.
9. Candy skeletons.
10. Figures of kings on camels.

Práctica escrita 4

Las celebraciones. The medical department where you work has asked you to jot down the days of the week, the date and month that the employees that you supervise will not be working.

Write out the dates.

1/11:
11/3:
27/6:
4/7:
2/4:
31/10:
28/11:
25/12:
13/1:

Práctica escrita 5

Contestar las preguntas con frases completas que incluyan las fechas:

1. ¿Cuál es la fecha de Navidad?
2. ¿Cuál es la fecha del día de San Valentín?
3. ¿En qué mes celebramos el Día de la Independencia?
4. ¿En qué meses son los cumpleaños de sus hijos?
5. ¿En qué mes estamos ahora?
6. ¿Cuál es la fecha de hoy?
7. ¿En qué fechas celebra su paciente el *Día de Muertos*?

Role-play 1

Look at the doctor's appointment book and play the part of the receptionist who calls the adult patients to remind them of their appointments.

Greet the patients by name and title.
Identify yourself as Dra. Ripoll González's receptionist.
Ask how they are feeling.
Inform the patients of the appointment date and time with the doctor (include a.m./p.m.).
Thank them.
Close.

Citas para la doctora Ripoll González

Miércoles	11/2	9:15	Sra. Martínez
Viernes	28/9	3:40	Srta. Ferrer
Viernes	16/11	12:00	Sr. Medina
Jueves	13/7	11:45	Sr. Roma
Martes	7/6	2:10	Sra. Nadal
Lunes	15/1	7:36	Srta. Castro
Jueves	21/3	8:20	Sra. Roca

C. Birthdates and birthdays

I. Birthdates

The word *nacimiento* refers to birth. To inquire about a birthdate, use the question:

¿Cuál es la fecha de su nacimiento? (Es el 13 de febrero de 1956)

2. Birthdays

The word *cumpleaños* means "birthday." As in English, do not provide the year of birth when giving the date of a birthday. There are several ways to ask questions about birthdays in Spanish:

¿Qué día es su cumpleaños? (Mi cumpleaños es el trece)
¿En qué mes es su cumpleaños? (Mi cumpleaños es en febrero)
¿Cuál es la fecha de su cumpleaños? (Es el 13 de febrero)

3. The verb (celebrar)

(Celebrar) is a cognate and a regular -ar verb. It can be used to talk about any celebration.

¿En qué mes celebra su cumpleaños? (Celebro mi cumpleaños en febrero)
¿En qué fecha celebramos la Navidad? (Celebramos la Navidad el 25 de diciembre)

Audio 3 (birthdays and birthdates)

Práctica oral 2

Los cumpleaños y los meses. Imagine that you are a receptionist at a pediatrician's office in a local hospital. This morning, one of the patients brings her 5 children to her medical appointment. The doctor has been detained and you reach out to the kids and ask them about their birthdays. Play the role of the receptionist with 5 classmates/children. *Circular por la clase y preguntar a 5 compañeros sobre el mes de su cumpleaños. Su compañero necesita contestar con una frase completa. Escribir el nombre inventado del niño en el mes apropiado.*

   Modelo: *¿En qué mes celebras tu cumpleaños? Celebro mi cumpleaños en abril.*

Mes	Nombre del niño o de la niña
enero	
febrero	
marzo	
abril	
mayo	
junio	
julio	
agosto	
septiembre	
octubre	
noviembre	
diciembre	

Práctica escrita 6

Información personal del paciente. Revisar la información y escribir las respuestas con frases completas.

Nombre	Apellidos	Fecha de nacimiento
María	Gil Blanco	23/6/1991
Blanca	Payeras Buades	12/12/1996
Jaime	Nadal Frau	1/11/2001
Marín	Truyols Ozonas	13/9/1956
Toni	Mendez Gual	10/7/2005
Mateo	Ferragut López	6/2/2002
Carla	López Sánchez	3/4/1980

1. ¿Cuáles son los apellidos de María?
2. ¿En qué mes es la fecha de nacimiento de Blanca?
3. ¿Qué día es el cumpleaños de Marín?
4. ¿En qué mes celebra Toni su cumpleaños?
5. ¿Cuántos años tiene Carla?
6. ¿Cuándo es el cumpleaños de Mateo?
7. ¿Cuál es la fecha de nacimiento de Jaime?
8. ¿Cuál es la fecha del cumpleaños de Carla?
9. ¿Cuál es la fecha de tu cumpleaños?

D. Personal patient information

I. Vocabulary. Personal information

¿Cuál es la fecha de su nacimiento?

¿Cuál es su estado civil?

Soltero:	(single)
Casado:	(married)
Separado:	(separated)
Divorciado:	(divorced)
Viudo:	(widowed)
¿Cuál es su peso?	(weight in *libras* "pounds")
¿Cuál es su altura?	(height in *pies* "feet" and *pulgadas* "inches")
¿Cuál es su sexo?	(*hombre* or *mujer*)
¿Cuál es su nacionalidad?	(*estadounidense, español*)
¿Cuál es su código postal?	(zip code)
¿Cuál es su prefijo?	(area code)

¿Cuál es el nombre y el número de su seguro médico?

¿Cuál es el número de su DIN o documento de identidad nacional?

◉ ¡OJO!

Nationalities are adjectives and are not capitalized; however, the proper names of countries are proper nouns and should be capitalized.

Argentina: argentino / a / os / as
Chile: chileno / a / os / as
Colombia: colombiano / a / os / as
Costa Rica: costarricense / s
Ecuador: ecuatoriano / a / os / as
El Salvador: salvadoreño / a / os / as
Guatemala: guatemalteco / a / os / as
Haití: haitiano / a / os / as
Honduras: hondureño / a / os / as

La República Dominicana: dominicano / a / os / as
México: mexicano / a / os / as
Nicaragua: nicaragüense / s
Panamá: panameño / a / os / as
Paraguay: paraguayo / a / os / as
Puerto Rico: puertorriqueño / a / os / as
Perú: peruano / a / o / os / as
Uruguay: uruguayo / a / os / as
Venezuela: venezolano / a / os / as

Audio 4 las nacionalidades

Conversación breve

A receptionist takes down some personal information of a patient, before her visit with the doctor.

—Buenos días, señorita. Tengo unas preguntas personales antes de su cita. ¿Cuál es su nombre completo?
—Mi nombre completo es Ángela Estriba Alonso.
—¿Cuál es la fecha de su nacimiento?
—Es el 15 de marzo de mil novecientos noventa.
—¿Cuál es su dirección?
—Mi dirección es calle Main 44, Cleveland, Ohio 44303.
—¿Tiene usted teléfono fijo?
—No, tengo celular solamente.
—¿Cuál es el número de su celular?
—Es el 982–3456.
—¿Cuál es el prefijo?
—Es 216.
—¿Cuál es su nacionalidad, señorita?
—Soy guatemalteca.
—¿Cuál es su estado civil?
—¿Perdón?
—¿Es usted casada o soltera, Ángela?
—Soy soltera.
—¿Tiene usted seguro médico?
—Sí. Aquí tiene mi tarjeta.
—¡Muchas gracias, señorita!
—¡No, gracias a usted!

Audio 5 información del paciente

Práctica escrita 7

Usted es el padre o la madre de una paciente joven. Completar la información para su hija:

INFORMACIÓN PERSONAL DEL PACIENTE

Madre____   Padre____   Comadre____   Compadre____

Sus apellidos: _____

Su nombre: _____

Nombre completo del paciente: _____

Edad:

Dirección: _____
                    (calle)   (número de casa)

_____
        (ciudad)   (estado)   (código postal)

Teléfono fijo de casa: (   ) _____

Tel. del trabajo: (   ) _____

Tel. celular: (   ) _____

Sexo: _____

Nacionalidad:

Compañía de seguro médico:

Número de grupo o póliza:

*En caso de emergencia notificar a _____ parentesco_____

Teléf. (   )_____

Cultura 2 (health insurance)

Some Hispanic patients may be afraid to seek health care because they don't have access to health insurance. While some families may have medical insurance, generally Hispanics have the highest rate of uninsured in the US. According to the CDC/National Center of Health Statistics, 21.4% or about 1 in 5 Hispanics under age 65 is uninsured. For those 65 and over, that number drops to 3.8%. The percentage of uninsured among Mexican/

Mexican Americans is higher still at 24.1% or roughly 1 in 4. The study defines "poor" Hispanic as those who have an income under the national poverty threshold. Accordingly, with "poor" Hispanics the percentage of uninsured rises to 32.7% or 1 in 3 (National Health Interview Survey, 2017). Undocumented immigrants are the least likely to access health services (Vargas et al., 2014). In addition, the kinds of jobs that Hispanics usually hold in the US, such as domestic, agriculture and food services, are less likely to offer health services. Despite some progress in access with the Affordable Care Act (ACA), Hispanics still have the lowest enrollment numbers compared to other minorities (Mosqueira et al., 2016). Without health insurance, health care can be unaffordable. The health provider or medical staff needs to be aware of the effect that the lack of insurance may have on their health practices and on the frequency of their patients' medical visits. Many patients will seek temporary solutions to their health issues at emergency rooms which do not provide follow-up care or preventive services (Chong, 2002).

Source: www.commonwealthfund.org/publications/blog/2016/jan/better-outreach-critical-to-aca-enrollment-particularly-for-latinos; https://ftp.cdc.gov/pub/Health_Statistics/NCHS/NHIS/SHS/2017_SHS_Table_P-11.pdf

Práctica escrita 8

Contestar las preguntas personales

1. ¿Cuál es su fecha de nacimiento?
2. ¿Cuál es su nacionalidad?
3. ¿Cuál es su estado civil?
4. ¿Cuál es su dirección?
5. ¿Cuál es su número de teléfono?
6. ¿Cuál es el número de su DIN?

Práctica oral 3

Entrevista. Hacer preguntas a un compañero. Usar las preguntas de la práctica 8.

Role-play 2

You are a receptionist in the pediatrics department and you want to take down some patient information before the first meeting takes place between a 15-year-old female patient and the doctor. Make sure that you vary the content of this role-play with different partners:

> Greet your patient appropriately.
> Introduce yourself.
> Ask for first and last names.
> Ask 3 additional patient information questions (birthdate, nationality, address).
> Ask about her general condition.
> Ask for 3 symptoms.
> Thank patient.
> Close the conversation.

Role-play 3

You are a receptionist in the pediatrics department and you want to take down some patient information before the first meeting takes place between the mother of an infant and the doctor. Make sure that you vary the content of this role-play with different partners:

> Greet your patient appropriately.
> Introduce yourself.
> Ask for mother and child's first and last names.
> Ask 3 additional patient information questions of your choice.
> Ask about child's general condition.
> Ask for 3 symptoms.
> Thank mother.
> Close the conversation.

Bibliography

Chong, Nida. "Defining the Latino Patient." *The Latino Patient.* Intercultural Press, 2002, pp. 3–10.

Krause, Neal, and Elena, Bastida. "Contact with the Dead, Religion, and Death Anxiety among Older Mexican Americans." *Death Studies*, vol. 36, no. 10, 2012, 932–948.

Mosqueira, Adrian Garcia B. et al. "Better Outreach Critical to ACA Enrollment, Particularly for Latinos." *Commonwealth. Fund Blog*, January 2016.

Schur, Claudia L. and Feldman, Jacob. "Running in Place: How Job Characteristics, Immigrant Status, and Family Structure Keep Hispanics Uninsured." Project HOPE Center for *Health Affairs*, May, 2001.

Timmins, Caraway L. "The Impact of Language Barriers on the Health Care of Latinos in the United States: A Review of the Literature and Language of Practice." *The Journal of Midwifery and Women's Health*, vol. 47, no. 2, 2010, 80–96.

Vargas, Bustamante Arturo et al. "Identifying Health Insurance Predictors and the Main Reported Reasons for Being Uninsured among US Immigrants by Legal Authorization Status." *The International Journal of Health Planning and Management*, vol. 29, no. 1, 2014, 83–96.

United States Centers for Disease Control and Prevention. *National Health Interview Survey. National Center for Health Statistics*. Web. 2017.

Vega, William A. et al. "Health Disparities in the Latino Population." *Epidemiologic Reviews*, vol. 31, 2009, 99–112.

Smith, Alexander K. et al. "Palliative Care for Latino Patients and their Families: Whenever We Prayed, She Wept." *Journal of the American Medical Association*, vol. 301, no. 10, 2009, 1047–1057.

Is your patient active? Talking about seasonal activities

LEARNING OUTCOMES FOR CHAPTER 7

Oral proficiency

Students will acquire the oral communicative skills that will allow them to appropriately interact in Spanish with their patients in the following ways:

- Describe and elicit descriptions about the seasons.
- Discuss patient's and family member's favorite activities.
- Describe and elicit responses about patient's seasonal activities and practices.
- Elicit response and respond to questions with regular -er and -ir verbs.
- Narrate in the present tense using -er and -ir verbs.
- Use expressions of frequency when narrating in the present tense.
- Ask and respond to questions using stem changing verbs (*jugar*) and (*dormir*).
- Describe and elicit descriptions about activities using verb (*hacer*).
- Offer suggestions using *es necesario* + infinitive.
- Advise using *es malo* + infinitive or *es bueno* + infinitive.

Cultural humility

Students will demonstrate an awareness of how to respond to patients with cultural humility when learning about the Hispanic culturally based concepts or practices of *marianismo* and *colectivismo*, and the impact they may have on exercise and physical activity for some Hispanic women from less acculturated communities.

A. Seasonal activities

1. The seasons

Like the days of the week and the months of the year, the seasons are never capitalized in Spanish. Use the definite article with the season (never with the months).

LAS CUATRO ESTACIONES

> El invierno: diciembre, enero, febrero,
> La primavera: marzo, abril, mayo,
> El verano: junio, julio, agosto,
> El otoño: septiembre, octubre, noviembre.

Audio 1 las estaciones

Práctica escrita 1

Los cumpleaños: Escribir el mes y la estación del cumpleaños de sus parientes o amigos:

Parientes / Amigos	El mes	La estación
mi madre		
mi padre		
mi hermano mayor		
mi hermano menor		
mi hermana		
mi esposo / a		
mi exesposo / a		
mi hijo / a		
mi hijastro / a		
mi mejor amigo / a		
mi abuelo / a		
mi compadre		

Práctica escrita 2

¿Qué estación es? Contestar con una frase completa:

1._____

2._____

3._____

4._____

5._____

6._____

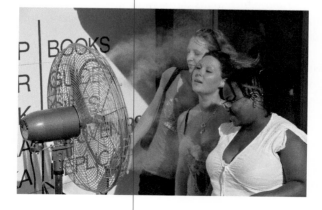

7._____

8._____

2. Talking about favorite seasons

To inquire about someone's favorite season use the question:

¿Cuál es su estación <u>favorita</u>?

Favorita is a cognate but it does not precede *estación* as it does in the English question or answer. As all descriptive adjectives do, it always follows the noun it describes:

Mi estación <u>favorita</u> es el verano.

Práctica oral 1 (en clase)

Actividad de grupo (7 personas). Imaginar que usted charla cordialmente con la familia de Juanito, un paciente de 10 años, después de una visita médica. Preguntar a la madre, el padre, la hermana de 21 años, el compadre y los abuelos paternos sobre sus estaciones favoritas.
En la primera columna, escribir la relación. En la segunda columna, su estación favorita con el artículo definido.
Después de la actividad, reportar a la clase.

Relación del familiar	Estación favorita
1.	
2.	
3.	
4.	
5.	
6.	

1. ¿Durante la actividad, cuántos miembros de la familia contestan "la primavera"?
2. ¿Quiénes son?
3. ¿Cuántos familiares contestan "el otoño" o "el verano"?
4. ¿Cuál es tu estación favorita?
5. ¿Hay familiares que contestan "el invierno"?
6. ¿Cuántos hay que contestan "el invierno"?

3. Vocabulary of seasonal activities

ACTIVIDADES DE TEMPORADA

Andar / montar en bicicleta	to ride a bike
Asistir a clases de inglés o a un concierto o escuchar un concierto	
al aire libre	outdoors
Bailar	to dance
Beber agua con o sin hielo (ice)	
Beber chocolate caliente	to drink
Caminar / andar en el vecindario	to walk
Comer muchas sopas calientes	to eat
Comer comida fresca	(not processed, frozen or canned).
Comer gazpacho (sopa fría)	
Comer helado	
Comer muchos dulces	
Correr en el parque o el gimnasio	to run
Cortar el césped (pasto o zacate)	to mow the lawn
Esquiar en la nieve	
Hacer sno (snowboard) hacer surf, yoga, ejercicios cardiovasculares / aeróbicos.	
Leer una novela en casa	
Levantar pesas	(weights)
Nadar en la playa o la piscina	to swim
Palear o quitar la nieve	to shovel snow
Pasear	to stroll
Plantar flores o vegetales	
Practicar deportes al aire libre	
Practicar el alpinismo, el tenis, el fútbol, el baloncesto, el golf, el béisbol	
Rastrillar las hojas	to rake leaves
Tomar un café o un refresco al aire libre o una siesta	
Tomar medicina para las alergias en la primavera	
Trabajar en la yarda	(garden / yard)
Trotar en la calle	to jog
Viajar	to travel

4. The activities and their prepositions

While you learn these new activities, review the following prepositions and their regular usage or meaning. In the parentheses you will find additional usages.

A: to (also used in a contraction with *el* in the expression *al aire libre*. When used with time / *hora*, *a* means "at" as in ¿A qué hora?)
CON: with
DE: of / from (also used to express a.m. / p.m. when telling time)
EN: in / at (also used with *montar* / *andar* **en** *bicicleta*)
POR: per (also used with **por** *la mañana, tarde, noche* when not telling time)

Audio 2 (seasonal activities) *actividades de temporada*

Conversación breve

—¿Cuál es su estación favorita, doña Antonia?
—Mi estación favorita es el verano, doctor.
—¿Por qué? ¿Qué hace usted en el verano?
—Pues, nado en la playa y monto en bicicleta los fines de semana. Algunas veces después del trabajo troto en la calle. Los viernes por la tarde siempre camino un poco a un café al aire libre con mi amiga. Allí, tomamos un refresco.
—¿Qué hace usted por la noche?
—Si hay fiesta, bailo con mis amigas en todas las estaciones.
—¡Muy bien, doña Antonia! Es muy saludable caminar y hacer actividad física con frecuencia.

Práctica escrita 3

Actividades de temporada y las estaciones. Write what season(s) patients would be likely to do these activities in Ohio, in Florida or in Maine.
    Modelo: *Comer helado: En Ohio, en el verano o en la primavera*

1. Trotar en la calle:
2. Comer muchas sopas calientes:

3. Nadar en la playa:
4. Esquiar en la nieve:
5. Caminar en el vecindario:
6. Trabajar en la yarda:
7. Practicar deportes al aire libre:
8. Cortar el zacate:
9. Tomar medicina para las alergias:
10. Palear nieve:

B. Regular -er / -ir verbs

Conjugating -er and -ir verbs.
   To form a regular -er or -ir verb in the present tense remove the -er or the -ir ending of the infinitive and add:

-o, -es, -e, -emos, -en	*for -er verbs*
-o, -es, -e, -imos, -en	*for -ir verbs.*

Note that they both share the same endings except for the "*nosotros*" form of -ir verbs.

(Comer) to eat
Yo como
Tú comes
El, ella, usted come
Nosotros comemos
Ellos / as, ustedes comen

(Vivir): to live
Yo vivo
Tú vives
El, ella, usted vive
Nosotros vivimos
Ellos / as, ustedes viven

Audio 3 (regular -er and -ir verbs) *verbos regulares -er y -ir*

Práctica escrita 4

Go back to the list of seasonal activities and organize them according to their conjugation type:

-ar	-er	-ir

I. Expressions of frequency

¿Con qué frecuencia? Adverbs of frequency indicate how often an activity occurs. These expressions can be placed at the beginning of the sentence or at the very end. If you place the negative expressions *nunca* and *casi nunca* at the end of the sentence, you must add a *no* before the verb: *No como dulces nunca / Nunca como dulces.*

Siempre / Nunca	Always / Never
Todos los días	Every day
Frecuentemente	Frequently
Algunas veces	Sometimes
Raramente	Rarely
Casi nunca	Hardly ever
Una vez, dos veces, etc., por día / semana.	Once, twice, etc., per day / per week

Audio 4 (expressions of frequency) *expresiones de frecuencia*

Práctica escrita 5

¿Con qué frecuencia hace estas actividades su paciente obeso de 42 años? Escribir frases completas y usar expresiones de frecuencia y las estaciones (la primavera, el verano, el otoño y el invierno):

  Modelo: Comer gazpacho. Mi paciente nunca come gazpacho en el verano.

1. Esquiar en el agua:
2. Trotar en la calle:
3. Viajar:
4. Cortar el zacate:
5. Comer muchos dulces:
6. Comer comida fresca:
7. Comer comida procesada:
8. Levantar pesas en el gimnasio:
9. Palear la nieve del estacionamiento de su casa:
10. Rastrillar las hojas en su yarda:

Práctica escrita 6

Conjugaciones. Completar con la forma correcta del presente del verbo en paréntesis:

Mi paciente don Esteban (vivir) _____ en Cleveland, Ohio. En el verano, su familia y él (nadar) _____ en la piscina de la casa del cuñado de don Esteban, porque ellos no (tener) _____ una piscina en su casa y tampoco tienen aire acondicionado. También algunos fines de semana, la familia (manejar) _____ con otras familias a un lago en Cleveland. En el lago, su esposa usualmente (leer) _____ y los tres niños, que son muy activos, (correr) _____ en la playa. El abuelo (tomar) _____ una siesta. Los Ramírez (ser) _____ una familia muy saludable. Siempre (beber) _____ agua con hielo y algunas veces (comer) _____ un helado al aire libre al final del día. Nunca (tomar) _____ coca-colas o bebidas de este tipo y no (comer) _____ muchos dulces, usualmente. Después del lago, (regresar) _____ a casa para cenar. En casa, ellos (cenar) _____ comida fresca y nunca procesada. Frecuentemente (comer) _____ gazpacho, una sopa fría de verduras frescas, o una buena ensalada. Después del trabajo y durante los fines de semana, don Esteban (trabajar) _____ en la yarda. El (cortar) _____ el zacate y su esposa doña Luisa generalmente (plantar) _____ flores o verduras. Doña Luisa (tener) _____ alergias y (tomar) _____ medicina cuando trabaja en la yarda. Algunas veces la familia (pasear) _____ en el vecindario. Los niños (montar) _____ en bici y los padres y el abuelo (andar) _____.

Práctica escrita 7

Write down 5 seasonal activities an unhealthy elderly patient does not do in the summer. Use expressions of frequency and your new -ar, -er and -ir verbs.

Práctica escrita 8

Preguntas de comprensión. Imagine that you are a healthy 21-year-old male patient. Answer these questions posed by the doctor, keeping his profile in mind.

1. En el verano, nada usted frecuentemente? ¿Dónde nada usted usualmente, en un lago o en una piscina? ¿Tiene usted una piscina en su casa?
2. ¿Trota usted en la calle en el invierno? ¿Cuántas veces por día? ¿Trota solo/a o con un amigo?
3. ¿Qué actividades físicas hace usted en el invierno? ¿Con qué frecuencia?
4. ¿Qué actividades físicas no hace usted en la primavera?

5. ¿Corta usted el zacate para sus padres en el verano?
6. ¿Qué come usted y bebe usted en el invierno?
7. ¿Cuándo rastrilla su padre las hojas en la yarda?
8. ¿Cuándo monta usted en bicicleta? ¿Con quién? ¿Dónde monta usted?
9. ¿Cuántas veces por semana corre usted en el gimnasio?
10. ¿Maneja usted mucho su carro o anda usted en bicicleta al trabajo en el verano?
11. ¿Quién palea la nieve del estacionamiento ("driveway" or "parking" area) en su casa en el invierno?

C. Stem changing verbs and verbs that change in the yo form

1. Conjugating stem changing verbs

(*Jugar*) "to play," (*dormir*) "to sleep" and (*sentir*) "to feel" are stem-changing verbs. Although their endings are regular, *jugar*: (*o, as, a, amos, an*) and *sentir* and *dormir*: (*o, es, e, imos, en*), these verbs have an additional change that occurs in the "stem" of the verb. The stem is the part of the verb that remains when you remove the -ar, -er and -ir endings of the infinitive.

jug-	*-ar*	*dorm-*	*-ir*	sent-	*-ir*
(stem)		(stem)		(stem)	

They are called stem-changing verbs because a vowel in the stem changes in a predictable way. In (*jugar*) the *u* in the stem changes to *ue* in all except the *nosotros* form of the verb. Similarly, in (*dormir*) the *o* changes to *ue* and in the verb (*sentir*) the *e* changes to *ie*. For these verbs the *nosotros* form, like the infinitive, does not have a change.

Jugar = *jugamos* dormir = *dormimos* sentir = sentimos
no stem change

The remaining verb forms have the stem change:

juego	*duermo*	*siento*
juegas	*duermes*	*sientes*
juega	*duerme*	*siente*
juegan	*duermen*	*sienten*

2. Conjugating verbs that are irregular in the yo form

The verb (*hacer*) is a regular -er verb except that is has a change or irregularity in the *yo* form: *Hago*.

(*Hacer*)
hago, haces, hace, hacemos, hacen.

3. Vocabulary of activities with verbs (jugar), (dormir), (sentir), *and* (hacer)

Jugar al fútbol, al béisbol, al baloncesto, al tenis, al golf.
Almo̱rzar (o changes to *ue) en la cafetería, en un café o restaurante, en casa.*
Dormir en el parque, al aire libre, en casa, la siesta.
Sentir is a synonym of *(tener)* when talking about symptoms.
Hacer yoga, ejercicios aeróbicos, ejercicios cardiovasculares, de estiramiento (stretching).

Audio 5 (stem changing verbs and verbs that change in the yo) *verbos de cambios de raíz y de cambios en el yo*

Cultura I (sedentarism)

Research indicates that sedentarism is associated with negative health outcomes and higher morbidity rates in Hispanic adults and children (Raynor, 2012). Excessive television viewing and working/playing on the computer can increase the risk of developing cardiovascular-related illnesses. In general, Hispanic subgroups have lower levels of leisure physical activity than non-Hispanic whites. Barriers to leisure physical activities can be socioeconomic, such as lack of access to facilities or of safe places to exercise, but lack of interest and self-discipline have also been reported as factors. Hispanic woman especially report lower levels of physical activity and suffer the negative health outcomes of sedentariness. Three out of every four Hispanic women are obese and will suffer from diabetes. Gendered cultural practices such as caregiving responsibilities and less social support or leisure time can negatively impact their involvement in physical activities (Larsen et al., 2013). *Marianismo*, a construct that describes a woman's position in the family and at home, dictates codes of behavior that prioritize family responsibilities over personal needs, particularly for women from less accultured groups. For them, exercising may be seen as an indulgence rather than a healthy practice. Dancing, however, is seen as a culturally appropriate form of physical activity and is culturally tied to the notion of *colectivismo* where life is viewed from a group perspective rather than a mainstream individualistic angle (Chong, 2002; D'Alonzo, 2012).

Práctica escrita 9

¿Qué hace(n)? Contestar con frases completas.

1. ¿Qué hace el tenista en el torneo?

2. ¿Qué hace ella en la playa?

3. ¿Qué hacen los niños en la piscina?

4. ¿Qué hacen estos atletas en el campeonato?

5. ¿Qué hace esta familia en la calle?

6. ¿Qué hacen estas personas con la música?

7. ¿Qué hacen ellas en el parque?

8. ¿Qué hacen ellos en el gimnasio?

Práctica escrita 10

Narración y descripción. Create a narration for the woman in the photograph. (A) Start with a description of what you see in the photo (*haber*) and describe the woman herself (name, nationality, family, civil status, personality). You will mostly use the verbs (*ser*) and (*tener*) in this section. (B) In the next section, identify the season or month and then narrate or tell what her typical activities are in that particular season using the present tense.

Role-play 1

You have an elderly 79-year-old patient with the following profile: he has a heart problem, diabetes and suffers from frequent dizzy spells. Additionally, he is severely obese. Ask him about his weekly activities and make sure to vary the content with each partner:

Greet him.
Ask him about his general condition.
Ask for some symptoms that would be relevant with his medical profile.
Ask 3 questions about his physical activities.
Follow up with a couple of frequency questions.
Ask one question about his meals.
Thank him.
Close.

At the end of the conversation, you will give him some "suggestions" using the expression *es necesario* + *infinitive* or some "gentle criticism" using *es malo*+ *infinitive* or *no es bueno* + infinitive or *debe / necesita* + infinitive. *Es necesario caminar todos los días. No es bueno beber cinco coca-colas por día, usted necesita comer comida fresca, usted no debe ser sedentario.*

Bibliography

Chong, Nida. "Defining the Latino Patient." *The Latino Patient*, 2002, pp. 3–10.

D'Alonzo, Karen T. "The Influence of Marianismo Beliefs on Physical Activity of Immigrant Latinas." *Journal of Transcultural Nursing: Official Journal of the Transcultural Nursing Society*, vol. 23, no. 2, 2012, 124–133.

Larsen, Britta A. et al. "Physical Activity in Latinas: Social and Environmental Influences." *Women's Health*, vol. 9, no. 2, 2013, 201–210.

Raynor, Hollie A. et al. "Sedentary Behaviors, Weight, and Health and Disease Risks." *Journal of Obesity*, vol. 2012, 2011, 1–3.

Discussing nutrition and healthy practices with your patients

---

LEARNING OUTCOMES FOR CHAPTER 8

Oral proficiency

Students will acquire the oral communicative skills that will allow them to appropriately interact in Spanish with their patients in the following ways:

- Discuss student's likes and dislikes using *gustar* + infinitive.
- Describe and elicit responses about likes and dislikes regarding exercise and nutrition.
- Describe and elicit responses about healthy and unhealthy practices with regards to nutrition, diets, sleep habits, exercise, and use of alcohol or drugs.
- Make recommendations using *es recomendable* + infinitive, *(no)es saludable* + infinitive.
- Describe or elicit information about places the patient regularly goes to in order to maintain healthy practices using *ir a* + place.
- Use *para* + infinitive for "in order to" when recommending places to a patient new to the area.

Cultural humility

Students will demonstrate an awareness of how to respond to patients with cultural humility when talking about their diets. While they should take into consideration that there may be an association between acculturation to mainstream US culture and negative dietary behavior for some Hispanics, they should not make a priori assumptions. Rather, they should specifically inquire about patients' personal dietary practices.

A. Talking about preferences using the valorative verbs (*disgustar*) and (*gustar*)

1. The verbs (gustar) *and* (disgustar) *to state preferences or dislikes*

The verbs (*gustar*) and (*disgustar*) are "valorative verbs." These verbs do not follow the regular "subject + verb + rest of the sentence" pattern. Although they mean "to like" or "to dislike," when used in Spanish they signify that something is dis(pleasing) to someone. The subject always follows these verbs, rather than preceding it.

The second unusual thing about these verbs is that they are not conjugated regularly.

Rather than having 5 forms, they only have 2 forms: (*dis*)*gusta* or (*dis*)*gustan*. The *a* ending is used if what follows (the subject) is a singular noun or an infinitive, while the *an* is used if what follows is a plural noun.

> *Me gusta dormir en el parque.* (Since the subject is the infinitive, *dormir*, the correct verb form for *gustar* ends with an *a*.)

> *Me disgusta el café.* (Since the subject is the singular noun, *el café*, the correct form for *disgustar* ends with an *a*. Note that you must always place the correct form of the definite article, an *el / la*, before the singular noun.)

> *Me gustan los dulces.* (Since the subject is a plural noun, *los dulces*, the correct form of the verb ends with an *an*. Note that you must place the appropriate form of the definite article, *los / las* before the plural noun.)

2. Subject pronouns and (gustar) *verbs*

Never use a "subject pronoun" [*yo, tú, usted(es), él, ella, ellos*] before valorative verbs. It already has a subject that follows the verb and is either a noun or an infinitive. You must use the "object pronouns" (*me, te, le, nos, les*) instead before the verb. Follow the formula below:

	Me
	Te
(A él / ella, a Ud.)	**Le gusta /* an + subject [infinitive, noun(s)]
	Nos
(A ellos / as, a Uds.)	**Les*

The object pronouns (*me, te, le, nos, les*) state "to whom it pleases or displeases" (to me, to you, to him / her or you singular formal, to us and to them or to you plural formal).

¡OJO!

Using a singular *le* or a plural *les* before (*gustar*) does not affect the form of the verb. You must pay attention to the subject that follows (*gustar*) in order to determine if you are going to use the *a / an* ending:

Les gusta el café. (It is *el café*, a singular noun, that determines the *gusta* ending. Not the *les*.)

 ## Audio 1 (*gustar*)

 ## Una conversación breve

Isabel a 14-year-old female patient talks to her doctor about her new diet.
—Hola, Isabel.
—Hola, doctor Pardo Nadal.
—¿Cómo va todo con tu nueva dieta?
—Muy mal, doctor. Me disgustan las verduras y las frutas.
—Es muy saludable comer verduras y frutas cuando tienes un problema de obesidad, Isabel. Tu madre prepara comidas muy saludables. ¿No comes en casa?
—No. Mis padres son vegetarianos, y a ellos les disgusta la carne. Me gusta comer en McDonald's con mis amigas porque me encantan las hamburguesas, doctor.
—Isabel, no es saludable comer mucha carne o comida con grasas. Necesitas continuar con tu dieta y hacer ejercicio también.
—¿Practicas algún deporte con tus amigas?
—Sí, doctor. Jugamos a los videojuegos.
—Isabel, los videojuegos no son deportes. Necesitas hacer ejercicio porque eres muy sedentaria.
—Sí, doctor.

 ## Práctica escrita 1

¿Le(s) gusta? Escribir sobre las preferencias de sus pacientes:

1. ¿A su paciente de 52 años, le gusta pasear en el vecindario? A él,
2. ¿A su paciente mayor, le gusta jugar al fútbol o dormir? A él,
3. ¿A su paciente diabética, le gusta comer dulces? A ella,
4. ¿A su paciente artrítico, le gusta estirar los músculos por la mañana? A él,
5. ¿A sus pacientes alérgicos, les gusta caminar en el parque en la primavera? A ellos,
6. ¿A su paciente anémica, le gusta comer carne? A ella,

7. ¿A la profesora, le disgusta nadar en el Mediterráneo? A ella,
8. ¿A su paciente alcohólico le disgustan las cervezas? A él,
9. ¿A su paciente obeso, le gusta comer hamburguesas de MacDonald's? A él,
10. ¿A su hijo cólico, le gusta el broccoli? A él,

Práctica escrita 2

Diálogos. Escribir dos diálogos entre un paciente y un profesional de salud. El primer paciente es una paciente de 12 años. El segundo paciente es un adulto de 52 años.

Práctica oral 1 (en clase)

Las preferencias de sus pacientes (grupos de 5). Usted es enfermera en el departamento de gerontología de su hospital y charla con 4 pacientes mayores entre 65 y 70 años (inventar nombres e identidades) sobre sus hábitos y preferencias. Escribir únicamente (only) *el nombre de los pacientes que responden afirmativamente con un "sí". Reportar a la clase.*

Actividades	Nombres de los pacientes que contestan "sí"
1. ¿A usted, le gusta plantar flores en la yarda?	
2. ¿Le gusta andar 20 minutos, 3 días por semana?	
3. ¿Le gusta beber agua?	
4. ¿Le gusta tomar coca-cola?	
5. ¿Le gusta comer fruta por la mañana?	
6. ¿Le gusta bailar?	
7. ¿Le gusta pasear en el vecindario?	
8. ¿Le gusta más comer fruta o dulces?	
9. ¿Le gusta hacer ejercicios cardiovasculares los fines de semana?	
10. ¿Le gusta dormir durante el día?	
11. ¿Le gusta rastrillar las hojas en el otoño?	
12. ¿Le gusta nadar en un lago?	
13. ¿Le gusta plantar vegetales?	
14. ¿Le gusta palear la nieve del estacionamiento de su casa, en el invierno?	
15. ¿Le gusta comer carne todos los días?	

Práctica escrita 3

¿Qué le gusta hacer? Las preferencias de su paciente en el hospital. Imaginar que usted es una paciente de 47 años. Tiene 3 hijas de 8, 10 y 13 años, respectivamente. Usted trabaja en un restaurante tres noches por semana y los fines de semana durante el día. Su madre cuida a sus hijas por las noches. Contestar las preguntas con frases completas sobre sus hábitos:
    ¿Qué le gusta hacer...

1. Los lunes al mediodía?
2. Los martes a las once de la mañana?
3. Los miércoles a las tres de la tarde?
4. Los sábados por la noche?
5. Los domingos por la mañana?
6. En la primavera?
7. En el invierno?
8. En el verano?
9. Después de sus clases de inglés?
10. El día del cumpleaños de una de sus hijas?

B. Healthy and unhealthy practices

1. Vocabulary of healthy and unhealthy practices

PRÁCTICAS SALUDABLES

Bailar
Beber café y alcohol con moderación.
Beber muchos vasos / botellas de agua regularmente.
Beber jugo de naranja con el desayuno.
Comer fruta o cereales como la avena (oatmeal) *por la mañana.*
Comer porciones pequeñas durante el día.
Comer verduras frescas o vegetales frescos regularmente.
Comprar ingredientes en mercados al aire libre o supermercados con productos orgánicos
Dejar de fumar o de drogarse
Dormir al menos 8 horas por noche.
Hacer actividad física (caminar, correr, pasear, hacer ejercicio, montar en bici).
Hacer meditación.
Preparar comidas sanas en casa.
Si es anémico: comer una dieta con carne o rica en verduras con hierro (espinacas).

Si es obeso: controlar el consumo de carbohidratos simples, de azúcar. Eliminar el consumo de comida chatarra por las noches antes de acostarse.

Si es diabético: controlar los carbohidratos en la comida, limitar el consumo de azúcar en general y usar insulina.

Si es vegetariano: comer una dieta rica en proteínas (legumbres, frijoles, garbanzos, lentejas.)

Si tiene problemas de corazón: controlar el colesterol y evitar o limitar el consumo de carne.

PRÁCTICAS NO SALUDABLES

Beber café y alcohol en exceso.

Consumir comida con mucha grasa (fat) como tocino (bacon) o salchichas (sausage) para el desayuno.

Comer comida enlatada (canned) o congelada (frozen).

Comer comida procesada.

Comer dulces y postres en exceso.

Comer frecuentemente o únicamente en restaurantes de comida rápida.

Comer porciones enormes.

Comer comida chatarra.

Comer por la noche antes de acostarse.

Fumar (tabaco).

No controlar la dieta, el consumo de azúcar, el colesterol o los carbohidratos.

No dormir.

Ser sedentario (jugar a los videojuegos, mirar televisión o navegar la red y las redes sociales — Facebook — excesivamente).

Tomar drogas o drogarse.

Audio 2 (healthy and non-healthy practices)
prácticas saludables y no saludables

Cultura 1 (nutrition)

Studies have shown that there is a direct association between acculturation and Hispanic nutrition and diets (Ayala et al., 2008; Mainous et al., 2006). For example, Mexican American adults born in rural areas of

Mexico follow healthier diets rich in vegetables, fruits and grains, and consume less fats and sugars. A higher acculturation to the US has been generally associated with a decrease in healthy diets and an increase in sugar intakes, in consumption of sugar-sweetened beverages and foods with added fats and low in fiber. Likewise, higher levels of acculturation have been associated with a higher frequency in eating out, at fast food restaurants. These findings support the position that health providers should protect positive dietary practices from the Hispanic countries of origin and improve the diets of more accultured groups (Pérez-Escamilla, 2011). However, recent research has maintained that due to the role of globalization and transnational modernization of the diets of Latin American countries, extant acculturation research is not always adequate to examine dietary change for immigrants who resided in urban areas in their countries of origin or migrated after 2000, because the chances are that they were also exposed to processed and junk foods (Martínez, 2013). While these finding are based on a study on relatively recent immigrants, from higher socioeconomic and predominantly urban backgrounds, it remains always important for healthcare providers to not make a priori assumptions about Hispanic diets. Rather they should inquire specifically about their patient's food purchasing practices, their sources of health information and their individual views on what it means to them to "eat healthy."

 ## *Práctica escrita 4*

Describir y narrar. Using 15 sentences, describe this young adult using what you see in the photo and your imagination (age, weight, nationality, physical characteristics, personality traits). Write about a day in his life and his (un)healthy practices. Create some sentences with the "valorative verbs" (*gustar*) y (*disgustar*) and other sentences with present tense verbs.

1.

2.

3.

4.

5.

6.

7.

8.

9.

10.

11.

12.

13.

14.

15.

Práctica escrita 5

Go back to the image in *Práctica* 4 and give your patient 6 suggestions using the expressions: *es necesario + infinitivo, (no) es recomendable + infinitivo, (no) es saludable + infinitivo*:

1.
2.
3.

4.

5.

6.

Role-play 1

You meet at the hospital cafeteria with a middle-aged female patient who you have known now for a long time and has become a friend. Discuss your interests by asking each other what you do during the different seasons, in the evenings and in the weekends. Incorporate time, place and time expressions in your conversation to make it as fluid and natural as possible.

Role-play 2

A 56-year-old female patient has high blood pressure. She meets with a nurse for the first time, to discuss health and daily routines.

> Nurse greets patient.
> Asks patient for her name and date of birth.
> Asks patient how she is feeling.
> Nurse asks the following questions:
>
>> Number of hours the patient works per week (*por semana*).
>> Number of hours the patient watches television on the weekends.
>> Number of hours the patient sleeps per night.
>
> Asks 2 questions about the patient's diet.
> Asks 4 questions about the patient's healthy practices.
> Nurse makes several recommendations.
> Nurse thanks patient.
> Conversation is closed.

Práctica escrita 6

Diálogo entre un paciente diabético y su enfermera. The nurse is checking up on the practices of her 38-year-old diabetic patient. Write a dialogue that includes initial greeting and introductions, questions about patients likes and dislikes, questions about daily practices, and final recommendations.

C. Going places. Maintaining healthy practices

1. The verb (ir)

El verbo (*ir*) is an irregular verb like (*ser*), (*estar*) and (*tener*). It does not follow the regular conjugation rules or patterns of -ar, -er or -ir verbs.

(IR)

Yo	*voy*
Tú	*vas*
El, ella, usted	*va*
Nosotros	*vamos*
Ellos, ellas, ustedes	*van*

2. The preposition a *and the verb* (ir)

Always use the preposition *a* "to" with the verb (*ir*) "to go" in order to indicate movement "toward" a place. Make sure that you pay attention to the gender of the place you are going to as you will have to use *al, a la, a los, a las* appropriately:

> *Antes de la clase, <u>voy **a la**</u> biblioteca. Después de la clase, <u>voy **al**</u> café.*

When *a* is followed by a possessive adjective, an article is not needed:

> *Después de la clase, generalmente <u>voy **a** mi casa</u>.*

Never use an article with a proper noun:

> *Los fines de semana <u>voy **a**</u> Cleveland.*

 Audio 3 el verbo (ir)

 Práctica escrita 7

Escribir la forma apropiada de a+ artículo definido para estos lugares:
   <u>Modelo</u>: *quiosco*:   *al quiosco.*

1. Sala de rehabilitación:
2. Oficina administrativa:
3. Unidad de recuperación:
4. Recepción:
5. Salida principal:
6. Ascensor amarillo:
7. Escaleras mecánicas:
8. Puente:
9. Supermercado:
10. Restaurante:

Práctica escrita 8

El verbo (ir). Escribir la forma correcta del verbo (ir) + a+ el artículo definido apropiado (al, a la, a los o a las):
    <u>Modelo</u>: *La recepcionista _____ servicios. La recepcionista <u>va a</u> los servicios.*

1. El paciente diabético _____ consultorio del diabetólogo.
2. El paciente enfermizo _____ sala de emergencias.
3. El paciente con dolor de pecho _____ centro de corazón.
4. La paciente con la pierna fracturada _____ ortopedia.
5. El paciente paranoico _____ cita con el sicólogo.
6. La enfermera _____ estación de enfermeras.
7. Los familiares del paciente _____ tienda de regalos.
8. El farmacéutico llega al hospital y _____ farmacia.
9. El médico _____ estacionamiento y aparca su carro.
10. El esposo de la paciente _____ unidad de maternidad.

Práctica escrita 9

Escribir 6 oraciones que describen su rutina en el hospital: las horas, los lugares en el hospital, el verbo (ir) + a y el artículo definido apropiado (a, al, a la, a los o a las).

Práctica escrita 10

Completar con la forma correcta de (ser), (estar), (tener) o (ir), según el contexto:

Mi prima Julia _____ enfermera en un hospital. Ella _____
joven, _____ casada y _____ 39 años. Su hijo _____ en
la universidad. Es muy popular y _____ muchos amigos. Julia
trabaja mucho y siempre _____ cansada porque ella _____
a su trabajo todos los días de la semana y también los fines de semana.
Su oficina _____ en un edificio muy moderno. _____
en Chicago. Ella y su vecina _____ al trabajo juntas (*together*)
porque las dos trabajan en una clínica. Hoy su hijo _____ muy
enfermo y _____ en casa. El _____ fiebre y _____
tos.

3. The preposition para

The preposition *para* means "in order to." *Para* is followed always by an infinitive when it has this meaning:

> *¿A dónde vas **para levantar** pesas? Yo voy al gimnasio **para levantar** pesas.*

Práctica escrita 11

¿A dónde va(n) para…? Write where the people go in order to do the following activities. Use *para* ("in order to") + infinitive:

1.

Modelo: *El atleta va a la piscina para nadar y para hacer ejercicio.*

2.

Los estudiantes _____

3.

Tú_____

4.

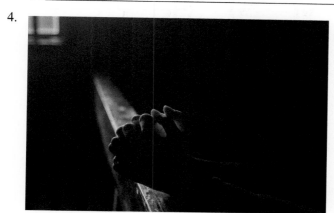

La familia del paciente_____

5.

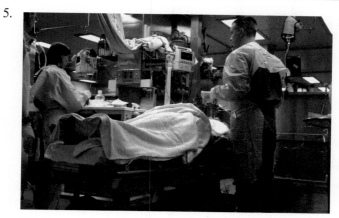

Ellos _____

6.

Nosotras _____

7.

El pediatra _____

 Práctica escrita 12

¿Qué hace usted para ser saludable? Answer these questions using *para +
infinitivo.*

1. Usted es diabético:

    ¿Qué hace usted para controlar su azúcar? ¿Qué come? ¿A dónde
    va para comer o comprar comida saludable?

2. Usted es obesa:

    ¿Qué hace para controlar su peso? ¿A dónde va para hacer ejer-
    cicio? ¿Para correr? ¿Para caminar? ¿Para hacer yoga o ejercicios
    cardiovasculares?

3. Usted tiene hipertensión y mucho estrés en su vida y su trabajo:

¿Qué hace para controlar su estrés?

 ### Role-play 3

The parent of a new patient has just moved to town. She is a health nut and likes to stay fit. She asks you about places she should go to locally in order to find healthy produce and maintain a healthy lifestyle. Vary your content with each partner:

After the usual introductions and greetings, the parent asks you where you go to buy your fresh organic vegetables, do yoga and eat vegetarian food. Answer her questions and provide addresses and general directions.

Bibliography

Ayala, Guadalupe X. et al. "A Systematic Review of the Relationship between Acculturation and Diet among Latinos in the United States: Implications for Future Research." *Journal of the Dietetic Association*, vol. 108, no. 8, 2008, 1330–1344.

Edmonds, Velma M. "The Nutritional Patterns of Recently Immigrated Honduran Women." *Journal of Transcultural Nursing*, vol. 16, no. 3, 2005, 226–235.

Mainous, Arch G. et al. "Acculturation and Diabetes among Hispanics: Evidence from the 1999–2002 National Health and Nutrition Examination Survey." *Public Health Reports (Washington, D.C.: 1974)*, vol. 121, no. 1, 2006, 60–66.

Martínez, Airín D. "Reconsidering Acculturation in Dietary Change Research among Latino Immigrants: Challenging the Preconditions of US Migration." *Ethnicity & Health*, vol. 18, no. 2, 2013, 115–135.

Pérez-Escamilla, Rafael. "Acculturation, Nutrition, and Health Disparities in Latinos." *The American Journal of Clinical Nutrition*, vol. 93, no. 5, 2011, 1163–1167.

Chapter 9

Talking about future plans and obligations with patients

LEARNING OUTCOMES FOR CHAPTER 9

Oral proficiency

Students will acquire the oral communicative skills that will allow them to appropriately interact in Spanish with their patients in the following ways:

- Describe and elicit responses from patients about future plans using (*ir*) *a* + infinitive and (*pensar*) + infinitive.
- Describe and elicit responses from patients using adverbial time expressions for the future.
- Narrate appropriately in the present and future about a health practitioner's daily routine in the hospital or a patient's plans for the weekend.
- Discuss preferences with patients using the infinitive constructions (*encantar*) + infinitive and (*preferir*) + infinitive.
- Discuss obligation with patients using (*tener*) *que* + infinitive, (*haber*) *que* + infinitive, (*necesitar*) + infinitive and (*deber*) + infinitive with regard to poor nutrition and generally unhealthy practices.
- Discuss places in the city with a new patient.

Cultural humility

Students will demonstrate an awareness of how to respond to patients with cultural humility when learning about the following Hispanic culturally based practice:

- Family cohesion and obligation values that lead members to be instrumental in assisting others with daily chores and activities.

A. The infinitive and its constructions

1. The infinitive's morphology.

The infinitive is the non-conjugated (non-personalized) form of the verb. In Spanish the infinitive is never used directly after a noun subject (person, place or thing) or a subject pronoun (*yo, tú, él/ella, usted, nosotros, ellos/ellas, ustedes*). Subject nouns or pronouns must always be followed by a conjugated verb with an appropriate, personalized verb ending:

2. Uses of the infinitive

    A. After a preposition (*a, de, en, para, por, con, sin* and *hasta*): *Voy al gimnasio para levantar pesas*

    B. After a conjugated verb in an infinitive construction: *Me gusta ir al gimnasio.*

3. Infinitive constructions

The infinitive is the most basic form of the verb and on its own does not indicate tense. When the infinitive is used in a construction with the verb (*gustar*), it expresses preference. When it is part of a construction with the verb (*ir*) and the preposition *a*, it expresses future plans "going to do."

    Me gusta viajar (preference)
    Voy a viajar el martes (future plans)

B. Future plans

1. Vocabulary of future time expressions

These temporal expressions are used to situate future action or plans in time:

Después de la clase, del trabajo
El año próximo
El fin de semana próximo
El mes próximo
El semestre próximo
El verano próximo
El viernes, el viernes próximo
Esta tarde, esta noche, este fin de semana
La primavera próxima
La semana próxima
Mañana
Pasado mañana

¡OJO!

When using the infinitive construction (*ir a + infinitivo*) with a reflexive verb (*levantarse, ducharse, llamarse*), the reflexive pronoun is placed either before the entire construction, or at the end and attached to the infinitive:

> *El se va a levantar a las seis* or *El va a levantarse a las seis.*

The verb (*ir*) "to go" can be used twice in the infinitive construction for future plans when talking about your future plans "to go somewhere," just as it would in English. See below:

Voy a leer una novela esta tarde	(I am going to read a novel this afternoon)
Voy a ir al dentista esta tarde.	(I am going to go to the dentist this afternoon)

 ### Audio I los planes futuros

 ### Una conversación breve

El doctor Sánchez y su paciente de 69 años, señor Antonio Gómez Ripoll, cordialmente charlan sobre los planes del fin de semana, después del examen médico.

—¿Qué va a hacer este fin de semana, doctor Sánchez?
—Pues, el sábado por la noche mi esposa y yo vamos a ir a un concierto de música clásica al aire libre. Nos encanta Bach. ¿Y usted, don Antonio?
—El sábado por la mañana voy a ir al gimnasio para hacer ejercicios cardiovasculares. Después, voy a almorzar en el centro con mi familia. Hay un nuevo restaurante mexicano.
—¡Excelente! Es muy saludable ir al gimnasio. ¿Cuántas veces por semana hace usted ejercicios cardiovasculares?
—Dos veces por semana después de trabajar y los sábados. ¿Usted también piensa ir al gimnasio este fin de semana, doctor?
—No, mi esposa y yo vamos a ir al parque para montar en bicicleta. ¡No nos gustan los gimnasios, pero nos encantan los parques!

 ### Práctica escrita I

Los infinitivos. Identificación. Below is a list of verbs. Some verbs are (a) in the <u>infinitive form</u> and others are (b) <u>conjugated</u>. Simply write "infinitivo" next to the infinitives. For the conjugated forms, pick one of these choices:

verbo conjugado regular "R", irregular "I", cambio de raíz "CR" or *cambio en el yo "Y"* depending on the way that they are conjugated. If you are unsure of the categories of any of the verbs, go back to Chapter 5 (Grammar C) and Chapter 7 (Grammars B and C).

<u>Modelos</u>: *Comer: infinitivo;*   *Hablar: regular "R"*

1. Tienen:
2. Es:
3. Estás:
4. Buscar:
5. Hacer:
6. Levantarse:
7. Llego:
8. Juega:
9. Hago:
10. Duermes:
11. Nadas:
12. Estirar:
13. Pensar:
14. Prefiero:
15. Vamos:

 Práctica escrita 2

Carefully review grammar points (A.2) and (A.3) in this chapter. These grammar points identify when to use the infinitive in Spanish. The infinitive is used after a preposition (*en, a, por, para, sin, con, hasta*) or after a conjugated verb. Identify the uses of the infinitive underlined below in each sentence by writing "infinitive" or "conjugated verb" next to the relevant sentence.

1. Me *disgusta* <u>comer</u> comida procesada.
2. Estudio español *para* <u>hablar</u> con mis pacientes hispanos.
3. A mi paciente hispano, *le encanta* <u>tomar</u> azúcar con su café.
4. El niño *prefiere* <u>beber</u> refrescos y no agua.
5. *Es saludable* <u>ir</u> al gimnasio para hacer ejercicio.
6. Los vegetarianos *prefieren* <u>controlar</u> el consumo de la carne.
7. No *es bueno* <u>beber</u> 5 coca-colas por día.
8. Me *gusta* <u>hacer</u> yoga en el parque.
9. Vas *a* <u>dormir</u> la siesta?
10. A los americanos, les *encanta* <u>comer</u> porciones enormes de comida.
11. Esta noche voy *a* <u>comprar</u> ingredientes frescos en el mercado.
12. Debes <u>hacer</u> meditación todos los días.

Práctica escrita 3

Planes futuros de los pacientes en su hospital. Write about the future plans of patients substituting these present tense verbs with the infinitive construction (*ir a+ infinitivo*) for the future and a variety of future time expressions:

1. El paciente enfermizo habla con su doctora hoy.
2. El paciente anémico come carne todos los días.
3. El niño obeso come muchos dulces y postres por la noche.
4. El paciente diabético controla sus niveles de azúcar cada día.
5. El paciente depresivo consulta con su psicólogo este martes.
6. El paciente alcohólico no bebe alcohol en su casa.
7. La niña alérgica no camina en el parque en la primavera.
8. El niño con cólico no come frijoles en el almuerzo.
9. El paciente sano monta en bici.
10. El nuevo paciente no fuma y juega al tenis los fines de semana.

Práctica escrita 4

Una conversación breve. Completar esta conversación entre la enfermera Ruiz y su paciente doña María, sobre los planes para el fin de semana:

—Doña María, qué _____ a hacer este próximo fin de _____?
—Voy a _____ al mercado para _____ comida. Tengo una cena en mi casa el sábado por la noche y necesito _____ los ingredientes.
—Ah, ¿le _____ cocinar?
—Sí, _____ encanta preparar comida sana para mi familia.
—¿A sus hijos, les _____ los vegetales, doña Luisa?
—A Tomas, le disgustan, pero _____ las legumbres. Mi hija es _____.
No come carne.
—Es bueno _____ una dieta rica en legumbres si no come carne.
—Sí, a ella le _____ los garbanzos, los frijoles y las lentejas.

Práctica escrita 5

Preguntas sobre el futuro. Después de un examen médico, el doctor charla con su paciente doña Isabel en su consultorio. Usted es doña Isabel. Contestar con la construcción infintiva para describir sus planes futuros. Usar su imaginación.

1. ¿Doña Isabel, a qué hora va usted a cenar esta noche?
2. ¿A qué hora <u>se</u> va a levantar mañana por la mañana? (Review the explanation above in ¡OJO! and give both possible choices of pronoun ("se"/"me") location in your answer.)
3. ¿A dónde va a ir usted después de esta visita al hospital?

4. ¿A qué hora va a terminar el trabajo el viernes?
5. ¿Qué va a hacer con su familia este fin de semana?

Práctica oral 1 (en clase)

Usted es la enfermera López. Preguntar a su paciente de 63 años, señor Lalo Alonso, sobre sus actividades el fin de semana próximo:

Pregunta	Respuesta	Reportar
1. ¿Qué va a hacer el sábado por la noche?	1.	1.
2. ¿A qué hora va a levantar**se** el próximo domingo?	2.	2.
3. ¿Va a visitar a un amigo o a un familiar este fin de semana?	3.	3.
4. ¿Qué actividad física va a hacer y con quién?	4.	4.
5. ¿Qué actividad no saludable va a hacer?	5.	5.
6. ¿Va a leer el periódico el domingo por la mañana? ¿Cuál?	6.	6.
7. ¿Va a desayunar en casa, en un café o en restaurante el domingo?	7.	7.
8. ¿Se va a duchar todas las mañanas?	8.	8.
9. ¿Va a navegar el internet para buscar información?	9.	9.
10. ¿Va a ir a la iglesia para escuchar una misa "mass" el domingo?	10.	10.

Después de preguntar, reportar las actividades de su paciente usando la forma de la tercera persona del singular.

Práctica oral 2 (en clase)

Nombre completo	Ocupación	Horario	Actividad
1. Luisa Rullán López	Paciente	Lunes	Hacer una cita
2. Antonio Prieto Escobar	Terapeuta	Dos veces por semana	Trabajar en terapia física
3. Antonio Pascual	Supervisora	A las 8:00 de la mañana	Desayunar en la cafetería
4. Tonina Gil	Cirujano	Abril	Viajar a NY
5. Paco Nadal Tellería	Farmacéutico	Todos los días	Estar en la farmacia
6. Isabel Truyols Orozco	Recepcionista	Por las mañanas	Conversar con pacientes

Práctica escrita 6

Descripción y narración. Describe the pediatrician and the patient in the image. (1) Use (*haber*), (*llamarse*), (*ser*) and (*tener*) in the <u>present tense</u> to talk about their names, physical traits and personality. (2) Talk about the doctor's routine work in the hospital using the <u>present tense</u> of regular verbs. (3) Conclude by talking about her <u>future plans</u> for the weekend.

Role-play 1

After a medical appointment with a patient who suffers from diabetes and obesity, you discuss his plans for a new healthier lifestyle. Ask him about future health plans around sleep, nutrition and exercise. Vary the content with each partner.

---

2. More infinitive constructions for preferences and future plans with (preferir) *and* (pensar)

Other infinitive constructions besides (*gustar* + *infinitivo*) or (*ir a* + *infinitivo*) can also be used to express preferences and future plans. Use (*preferir* + *infinitivo*) to speak about your preferences and (*encantar* + *infinitivo*) to speak about what you "love" to do. Use (*pensar* + *infinitivo*) to talk about your future plans or what you are "planning" to do in the future.

(*Notice that *encantar* is a "valorative" verb and follows the structure of "gustar," while *preferir* and *pensar* are conjugated regularly as stem changing verbs.)

Preference	Future plans
Encantar + infinitive	*pensar (stem changer e>ie) + infinitive*
Preferir + infinitive (e>ie)	

Me encanta comer comida fresca. (preferencia)
Prefiero hablar con médicos hispanos. (preferencia)
Pienso acompañar a mi madre a su cita con el médico mañana. (planes futuros)

C. Obligations

1. Expressing obligation with (tener que), (hay que), (necesitar) *and* (deber)

To express obligation in Spanish, use the following infinitive constructions (Remember that in infinitive constructions the first verb must be conjugated. Here the exception is *"hay"* because it is an invariable verb that only has one form):

Deber + infinitivo
Hay que + infinitivo
Necesitar + infinitivo
Tener que + infinitivo

Debo comer fruta una vez por día.	(I ought to eat fruit once a day.)
Hay que beber 6 vasos de agua diariamente.	(One has to drink 6 glasses of water daily.)
Necesita descansar.	(You need to rest.)
Tenemos que caminar frecuentemente.	(We have to walk frequently.)

*The verb (llevar) is used to say that one is taking someone to a specific destination:

Debo llevar a mi abuela a la clínica.	(I have to take my grandmother to the clinic.)

Audio 2 *construcciones infinitivas de preferencia, planes futuros y obligación*

Cultura I (family cohesion and obligation values)

In Hispanic communities there is generally a strong sense of family cohesion and interdependence because of the central role of *familismo*. Many members of these communities are more family-oriented than individual-oriented and will act as strong support systems for their elders. Often, they will hold strong family obligation values and will be instrumental in assisting their parents or elders in daily activities such as child care, cooking and house cleaning, particularly because they may live in multi-generational homes. They may also be responsible for transporting elders that don't drive to the store, translating for them, or accompanying them to their appointments. Lastly, the role of caregiving for the elderly frequently will fall on the women in the family. However, it is important to keep in mind that family functioning and obligation values may vary or change generationally as a result of acculturation or acculturative stress (Ibañez et al., 2015).

Práctica oral 3 *(en casa y después en clase)*

Obligaciones. *Hacer sugerencias* "suggestions" *usando expresiones de obligación para estos pacientes:*

Paciente 1. Tengo 33 años y soy obeso. Me encanta mirar televisión por la noche y durante todo el fin de semana. Durante la semana duermo 4 horas por noche, porque miro televisión toda la noche. No me gusta beber agua y prefiero beber Coca-Cola o café por la noche. Necesito mucha cafeína porque siempre estoy cansado. Me levanto a las 7:00 de la mañana para ir a mi trabajo. Me disgustan las verduras y las frutas pero me encantan los postres y el azúcar.

Paciente 2. Tengo 17 años y tengo muchos problemas con mi familia. No me gusta estudiar y tengo malas notas en la escuela. Soy muy popular y me encanta ir a fiestas con mis amigos. En las fiestas hablamos con chicas y bebemos cerveza. Los fines de semana fumamos marihuana también y a veces nos drogamos en las discotecas o clubes cuando vamos a bailar.

Práctica oral 4 (en clase)

Entrevistar a un paciente:

<u>Interview</u> a classmate who is playing the role of señor Fernández a 36-year-old male patient. Use the present tense and a variety of infinitive constructions (10 sentences) to ask your questions. Be ready to report information about your "patient" to the class:

A. First, ask 5 questions about his family, work, habits and hobbies during particular times, seasons or dates. Use the present tense.

B. Then, ask 5 questions about his preferences (using *preferir+ infinitivo* and *encantar + infinitivo*) and his familial obligations using the infinitive constructions (*deber + infinitivo* and *tener que + infinitivo*).

D. Places in the city

1. Vocabulary of places in the city

LOS LUGARES EN LA CIUDAD

El almacén (Target, Macys etc.)
El banco, el cajero automático (depositar, sacar, cambiar dinero, pagar cuentas)
El bar / El café
El centro comercial (ir de compras, comprar)
El cine (ver una película) (ver es un verbo de cambio en el yo: **veo***, ves, ve…)*
El colegio, la escuela
El hospital
El hotel
El mercado al aire libre
El museo (mirar arte)
El parque (pasear)
El restaurante
El supermercado
El teatro (ver una obra de teatro)
El zoológico (pasear con la familia, ver animales)
La biblioteca (sacar o devolver libros) (devolver es un verbo de cambio de raíz o>ue)
La clínica
La comisaría (la policía)
La estación de trenes (esperar, tomar el tren)
La fábrica
La gasolinera (poner gasolina en el coche) (poner es un verbo de cambio en el yo: **pongo***, pones, pone, ponemos, ponen)*

La iglesia
La oficina de correos (cartas / sellos)
La parada de autobús, de taxis
La peluquería (lavarse el pelo, cortarse el pelo o la barba)
La tienda: La carnicería, la zapatería, la panadería (pan, dulces), la
  librería o la papelería (papel, lápices, libros, cuadernos)
La tintorería (llevar la ropa sucia y recoger la ropa limpia y planchada)
  (recoger "to pick up" es un verbo de cambio en el yo: recojo, reco-
  ges, recoge, recogemos, recogen)
La universidad

Audio 3 *lugares en la ciudad*

¡OJO! Librería is a false cognate. It does not mean library, but rather bookstore. Library in Spanish is *la biblioteca*.

Práctica escrita 7

Los lugares en la ciudad. ¿A dónde van a ir o piensan ir y para qué?
  Modelo: Yo / (cajero). *Yo pienso ir al cajero para sacar dinero.*

1. La madre:

2. La enfermera:

3. Mi hijo:

4. La doctora:

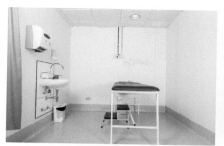

5. El paciente y su madre:

6. La familia:

7. Mi abuela:

8. Mi esposo:

9. Los criminales:

10. La cocinera:

11. El cartero:

12. Ustedes:

13. Mi tío:

14. Juan y su hijo:

15. El director:

16. Los atletas:

17. Los estudiantes:

Actividad oral 4 (en clase)

Obligaciones y planes después de la consulta con el médico (Grupos de 4). Usted es la recepcionista de la cardióloga doctora Isbert. Después de la consulta con el médico, usted charla con su paciente de 29 años, doña Antonia, y con dos miembros de su familia (el esposo: don Jaime y la hermana mayor de su paciente: señorita Ascorbe) sobre sus planes y obligaciones después de la consulta y durante el fin de semana.

Actividades	Nombre del paciente, su esposo o su hermana
¿Tiene que ir al supermercado esta tarde?	
¿Piensa ir de compras en el centro comercial el fin de semana?	
¿Va a cenar en un restaurante hoy?	
¿Piensa manejar a su casa?	
¿Necesita comprar gasolina para su coche en la gasolinera?	
¿Va a sacar dinero del cajero automático?	
¿Hay que devolver un libro a la biblioteca?	
¿Va a buscar ropa limpia a la tintorería?	
¿Piensa ver una película en el cine el sábado por la noche?	
¿Debe ir a casa de una amiga?	
¿Tiene que ir al dentista pronto?	
¿Necesita volver a la oficina mañana?	
¿Va a mirar un vídeo en casa con su familia?	

Práctica escrita 8

Actividades de don Luis. La enfermera Ruiz charla con su paciente de 43 años, don Luis. Usted es don Luis. Contestar a las preguntas con imaginación y usar el vocabulario de la ciudad también.

1. ¿A dónde va cuando necesita gasolina? *cuando (when)
2. ¿A dónde prefiere ir para comprar comida?
3. ¿Alguien en su familia trabaja en una fábrica? ¿Qué tipo de fábrica? ¿Quién es?
4. ¿A dónde debe ir para comprar cartas y sellos?
5. ¿A dónde le gusta ir a usted en la primavera?
6. ¿A dónde debe llevar a su madre los sábados por la mañana?
7. ¿A dónde debe ir cuando va a tener una cena en su casa?
8. ¿A dónde va a ir cuando alguien invade o roba su casa?
9. ¿A dónde lleva a sus padres para sus citas con el médico?

Práctica escrita 9

<u>Composición</u>. *Imaginar que usted es Leticia, una paciente de su hospital. Usted tiene 45 años y tiene un esposo, don Miguel, y dos hijas de 19 y 15 años: Sarita y Maya. Su madre tiene 70 años y tiene diabetes. Escribir una composición de*

10 oraciones sobre sus planes con su familia y sus obligaciones familiares para el fin de semana próximo. Usar una variedad de verbos diferentes y el vocabulario nuevo de la ciudad. Usar su imaginación.

Práctica escrita 10

Un hispano en Akron. You have a new Hispanic patient and meet his family. They have moved to Akron and don't know much about the city. Write a dialogue between you and them. Ask them what they like to do using infinitive constructions of preference, ask them what they need to do for their familial obligations and then describe places in Akron where they can do these activities using (*tener*) and (*haber*).

Role-play 2

Using the dialogue that you created in the previous exercise, dramatize a role-play with a classmate. Vary the contents of the simulation with new partners.

Bibliography

Flores, Yvette G. et al. "Beyond Familism: A Case Study of the Ethics of Care of a Latina Caregiver of an Elderly Parent with Dementia." *Health Care for Women International*, vol. 30, no. 12, 2009, 1055–1072.

Gallant, Mary P. et al. "Chronic Illness Self-Care and the Family Lives of Older Adults: A Synthetic Review across Four Ethnic Groups." *Journal of Cross-Cultural Gerontology*, vol. 25, no. 1, 2010, 21–43.

Ibañez, Gladys E. et al. "Changes in Family Cohesion and Acculturative Stress among Recent Latino Immigrants." *Journal of Ethnic & Cultural Diversity in Social Work*, vol. 24, no. 3, 2015, 219–234.

Chapter 10

Establishing a rapport with a new patient

LEARNING OUTCOMES FOR CHAPTER 10

Oral proficiency

Students will acquire the oral communicative skills that will allow them to appropriately interact in Spanish with their patients in the following ways:

- Describe and elicit descriptions from patients about the weather as conversation openers.
- Discuss and compare weather-related activities in the US and in their country of origin.
- Use exclamations with verbs, nouns and adjectives to talk about the weather conditions using ¡Qué!
- Describe and elicit descriptions about clothing using the verb *llevar*.
- Discuss clothing in the context of the weather, seasons and exercise.
- Compliment patient's clothing or family member's traits using ¡Qué + adjective! ¡Qué + adverb! and ¡Qué + noun + más/tan + adjective!

Cultural humility

Students will demonstrate an awareness of how to respond to patients with cultural humility when learning about the following Hispanic culturally based concepts or practices:

- The culturally based concept of *simpatía*.
- The interpersonal benefits of using conversation openers about the weather, clothing and family members to ease possible tension with new patients.

A. Conversation openers. The weather

1. ¿Qué tiempo hace hoy? Hoy hace sol.

When describing the weather, use the verb "hacer":
Hoy hace sol.
Never use (*hacer*) when you are saying that:

(1) it is snowing	(Nieva)
(2) it is raining	(Llueve)
(3) It is cloudy	(Está nublado or hay nubes)
(4) It is foggy	(Hay neblina)
(5) There is a storm	(Hay tormenta)

In the above weather descriptions, you use the appropriate verbs: "*nevar*," "*llover*," "*estar*" and "*haber*," but never "*hacer*."

2. Vocabulary of weather expressions

> *Hace (mucho, un poco de) calor* (it is hot out) / *hace frío* (it is cold) / *hace fresco* (it is chilly)
> *Hace (mucho / un poco de) viento* (it is windy)
> *Hace (mucho / poco) sol* (it is sunny)
> *Hace (muy) buen tiempo* (it is nice out) / *Hace mal tiempo* (it is is bad out)
> *Hace (mucha / poca) humedad* (it is humid)

> *Hoy nieva* (it is snowing)
> *Hoy llueve* (it is raining)
> *Hoy está nublado* (it is cloudy)
> *Hoy hay nubes* (there are clouds), *neblina* (fog), *tormenta* (storm) *y mucha humedad.*

Audio 1 (the weather) el tiempo

Práctica escrita 1

Leer las descripciones e identificar la estación correcta:

1. Nieva, hace mucho frío y hace muy mal tiempo.
2. Hace sol y todos van a nadar en la piscina.
3. Es el mes de octubre y hace mucho viento y un poco de fresco.

4. Hace mucho calor en el hospital, pero las enfermeras nunca llevan sandalias.
5. El esposo de mi paciente lleva botas porque llueve mucho hoy.
6. Hace mal tiempo todos los días y la temperatura mínima va a ser de 20 grados Fahrenheit.
7. No vamos a ir a la playa porque está muy nublado hoy.
8. El esposo de mi paciente lleva pantalones largos y un suéter.
9. Los hijos de mi paciente llevan pantalones cortos y sandalias.

 ### *Práctica escrita 2*

¿Qué tiempo hace en estos dibujos? Use as many weather expressions as you can to describe each image.

1.

2.

3.

4.

5.

6.

Práctica escrita 3

¿Qué tiempo hace y qué les gusta hacer? Describir el tiempo y decir las preferencias de cada persona. Usar gustar, preferir, disgustar y encantar.

1.

2.

3.

4.

5.

6.

7.

8.

Práctica escrita 4

Conversación con Dr. Alonso. Usted es un paciente del cardiólogo y conversa con el médico sobre el tiempo, después de su cita. Contestar las preguntas de Dr. Alonso con frases completas:

1. ¿Qué tiempo hace en su país (en México, en la República Dominicana, en Puerto Rico) en el invierno?
2. ¿Qué tiempo hace hoy?
3. ¿Le gustan las tormentas?
4. ¿Qué tiempo hace en su ciudad natal en Navidad?
5. ¿Quién en su familia palea la nieve del estacionamiento en su casa cuando nieva mucho?

B. Exclamations and icebreakers

1. Exclamations with verbs

Like interrogatives or question words, exclamations have written accent marks. When making an exclamation with a verb, use ¡*Cómo!* or ¡*Cuánto / a / os / as!* for "how" or "how much":

> ¡*Cómo llueve hoy, esta mañana, esta tarde!*   ¡*Cuánto llueve!*
> ¡*Cómo nieva esta semana, este invierno!*   ¡*Cuánto nieva!*

2. Exclamations with nouns or adjectives

When making an exclamation with an adjective, use ¡*Qué!* to mean "how" or "how much" it is.

> ¡*Qué lluvioso (soleado, nublado, húmedo, seco)!*
> ¡*Qué humedad (frío, calor, viento, sol, neblina, lluvia, sequía:* "What a drought")!

3. Exclamations with nouns and adjectives

When making an exclamation with a noun and an adjective use *más* or *tan* between the noun and adjective to mean "what a...very..."

> *¡Qué día (tiempo, mes, año, fin de semana) más / tan caluroso (frío, húmedo, seco, nublado)!*
> *¡Qué mañana (tarde, noche, semana) más / tan soleada, esplendida!*

Audio 2 los exclamativos

Una conversación breve

—Buenos días, don Luis.
—Buenos días, enfermera Ruiz Delgado.
—¡Qué tiempo tan terrible! ¿Verdad?
—Sí. ¡Cómo nieva y qué frío!
—¿Nieva en la República Dominica en el invierno, don Luis?
—En mi pueblo no. Algunas veces nieva así en las montañas.
—¿Qué tiempo hace en el verano?
—En el verano hace mucho calor y hay mucha humedad.

Práctica escrita 5

Exclamaciones y el tiempo. Completar con la(s) palabra(s) exclamativa(s) correcta(s):

1. ¡_____ semana _____ terrible!
2. ¡_____ invierno _____ frío!
3. ¡_____ llueve!
4. ¡_____ día _____ nublado!
5. ¡_____ tiempo _____ húmedo!
6. ¡_____ sol _____ intenso!
7. ¡_____ viento _____ fuerte!
8. ¡_____ nieva!

Práctica escrita 6

Escribir exclamaciones apropiadas a las situaciones. Write all of the possible exclamatory comments for the following situations:

1. It is frigid cold weather and has been like that all month.
2. Finally, the first sunny day in a long time.

3. It is August and the humidity is intolerable.
4. It has been raining nonstop and there is flooding in the city.
5. It has been an unbearably hot week.
6. There has been a drought this summer.

 ### Role-play 1

One morning in early December, you meet a new 63-year-old female Hispanic patient who seems a little tense. Make some initial small talk to ease the tension.

> Greet your patient.
> Introduce yourself.
> Make a comment about the amount of snow today.
> Patient agrees and says something about the temperature.
> Ask her what her nationality is.
> Ask her what the weather is like in December in her country.
> Ask about an activity that she likes to do when it snows.

Chile	chileno / a
Puerto Rico	puertorriqueño / a
México	mexicano / a
Honduras	hondureño / a
República Dominicana	dominicano / a
Paraguay / Uruguay	paraguayo / a-uruguayo / a
Cuba	cubano / a
Guatemala	guatemalteco / a

*Make sure you vary the content (weather expressions, months and origin) with each partner.

 ### Role-play 2

It is a dry very hot summer afternoon and you have a new very shy 13-year-old male Hispanic patient. Make some initial small talk to ease the tension.

> Greet your patient.
> Introduce yourself.
> Make a comment about the heat.
> Patient agrees and says something about the lack of rain.
> Ask him about his nationality.
> Ask him what the weather is like in July in his country.
> Ask about an activity that he likes to do when it is hot.

C. Clothing

I. El verbo (Llevar)

The regular verb (*llevar*) to wear is used to talk about clothing:

> *¿Qué ropa lleva la enfermera? Ella lleva pantalones cortos y sandalias.*

2. Uso y omisión de artículo indefinido con la ropa

The indefinite article *un / una* is used to talk about clothing if it is a singular item of clothing:

> *La paciente lleva **un suéter.***

When talking about plural items of clothing (shoes, pants, gloves, etc.), the indefinite article is omitted:

> *Los hijos de mi paciente llevan **pantalones de mezclilla y sandalias.***

3. Vocabulary of clothing

Arriba:

Un chaleco	a vest
Un polo	
Un suéter	
Una blusa (con botones para mujeres)	a blouse
Una camisa (con botones para hombres y mujeres)	a shirt
Una camiseta (*una playera)	a t-shirt
Una chaqueta (*una chamarra)	a jacket
Un saco de vestir	a blazer
Una sudadera	a sweat shirt

Abajo:

Leggings (*mallones)	
Pantalones	pants
Pantalones cortos	shorts
Una falda	a skirt
blue jeans (*pantalones de mezclilla)	jeans

Una pieza ("one-piece"):

Un abrigo	a coat
Un bañador (*un traje de baño)	a bathing suit
Un camisón (*una bata de dormir)	a nightgown
Un mono (*unos overoles)	a jumpsuit

Un pijama	
Ropa quirúrgica	scrubs
(*Filipinas)	scrub top
Un traje	a suit
Un uniforme	
Un vestido	a dress
Una bata	a robe

En los pies:

Botas	
Sandalias	
Zapatos atléticos	
Zapatos de tacón	high heels
Zapatos planos	flats

En la cabeza:

Un casco	a helmet
Un gorro	a cap
Un tapaboca (*una mascarilla)	surgical mask

Accesorios:

Anillos	rings
Calcetines	socks
Un estetoscopio	
Guantes	gloves
Lentes (lentes de contacto o lentillas)	
Medias	tights/hose
Pendientes o aros (*aretes)	earrings
Un bolso	
Un cinturón	a belt
Un collar	a necklace
Un pañuelo	a scarf
Un reloj	
Una bufanda	a heavy winter scarf
Una corbata	a tie
Una mochila	a book bag
Una pajarita (*un moño)	a bow tie
Una pulsera	a bracelet

Ropa interior:

*Un sujetador (*un brasier)*	a bra
*Unas bragas (*una pantaleta o un panti)*	female underwear
calzoncillos	male underwear

*Depending on the Hispanic country of origin, different terms may be used to refer to a particular item of clothing. The words in the vocabulary that are preceded by an asterisk are Mexican or Mexican American terms.

 ¡OJO!

In Spanish, "clothing" (*la ropa*) is a singular feminine collective noun like *la familia*. The definite article that accompanies a noun determines its gender and number.

 Audio 3 la ropa

 Práctica escrita 7

¿Qué ropa llevan ellos? Escribir descripciones completas de la ropa. If there is more than one person in the image, use adverbs of description in Spanish to indicate who you are talking about. For example, the women on the left (review Chapter 4. B-1).

1.

2.

3.

4.

Práctica escrita 8

La ropa y las actividades. Responder a la preguntas. Start your answer referring to the situation or context given using *Cuando + verb* / "When I" to begin your answer:

> Modelo: ¿Qué ropa llevas <u>cuando nadas</u>? Cuando nado, yo llevo .....

1. ¿Qué ropa llevas cuando examinas a un paciente?
2. ¿Qué ropa llevan las personas cuando esquían?
3. ¿Qué ropa llevamos por la noche cuando vamos a dormir?
4. ¿Qué ropa lleva usted cuando monta en bicicleta?
5. ¿Qué ropa lleva un tenista?
6. ¿Qué ropa llevas cuando vas a un restaurante elegante?
7. ¿Qué ropa llevas en la primavera?
8. ¿Qué ropa llevamos todos en el invierno?
9. ¿Qué ropa lleva un cirujano cuando va a operar?
10. ¿Qué ropa lleva una enfermera usualmente?
11. ¿Qué ropa lleva un paciente cuando tiene un examen físico?

Role-play 3

El campamento. A summer camp is coming up at your local hospital for children with diabetes. One of the parents of your 8-year-old patient wants to know what items the child will need to take to the camp. She calls you on the phone to ask. Use the vocabulary of clothing and the infinitive constructions of obligation.

> Greet your patient warmly.
> Ask how she is doing.
> Make a comment about the weather.
> Patient asks what clothing her daughter needs to take in order to attend the camp.
> You tell her.
> She thanks you.
> You close the conversation.

D. Complimenting with exclamations

I. La ropa y la descripción

Exclamaciones. When complimenting someone on their clothing, looks or personality use:

> *¡Qué + adjetivo! ¡Qué guapa (bonita, alta, delgada, simpática, extrovertida, inteligente, generosa, activa etc)!*
> *¡Qué + adverbo! ¡Qué bien* (nice), *divertido* (fun)!
> *¡Qué + nombre +más / tan+ adjetivo! ¡Qué vestido más elegante llevas!*
> *¡Qué noticia tan buena!*

Cultura I (simpatía)

Hispanics as a whole tend to be more focused on relationships than US Americans and may read the neutral or businesslike affect of a non-Hispanic health provider as a negative sign of lack of interest or detachment. Physical gestures or friendly comments that communicate warmth increase the likelihood of a trusting relationship between the Hispanic patient and the health provider. However, for some Hispanics who believe in the evil eye, complimenting may cause harm to befall someone and can be associated with jealousy. When parents believe in it, it may be helpful to touch a baby/child when admiring them, so as to avoid the perception that you are giving the evil eye. It is important to carefully read the reactions or cues of patients or family members when you compliment.

Source: www.jpeds.com/article/S0022-3476(00)90043-X/fulltext

Role-play 4

You are conversing with a 36-year-old parent about his 10-year-old child who spends too much time playing video games. The good news is that he has lost weight and has started to bike. You ask about this weekend plans and activities.

> Greet your patient and his mother.
> Ask the mother how she is doing.
> Make an opening comment about the weather.
> Ask the boy what he is *planning to do* this weekend.
> The boy responds that he is *going to ride* his bike in the park, close to his house with his friends because today is his birthday.
> Congratulate him on his birthday, on his bike and on his activity. Use a complimentary exclamation.
> Ask about his friends. How many friends live close by? What are their names and ages?
> Ask him what they usually wear when riding a bike.
> Child answers but does not mention a helmet.
> Recommend that he always wear a helmet.
> Remind the mother that wearing a helmet is very important.
> Mother agrees and thanks you.

Bibliography

Gropper, Rena C. *Culture and the Clinical Encounter. An Intercultural Sensitizer for the Health Professions.* Intercultural Press, Inc. 1996.

Conducting a physical examination

LEARNING OUTCOMES FOR CHAPTER 11

Oral proficiency

Students will acquire the oral communicative skills that will allow them to appropriately interact in Spanish with their patients in the following ways:

- Comprehend instructions and give instructions for a physical medical examination using both reflexive and non-reflexive verbs in the present tense.
- Comprehend commands and give commands using the constructions *favor de* + infinitive.
- Describe and elicit descriptions of types of pains.
- Describe and elicit descriptions of location of the pain.
- Discuss medication intake and dosages.
- Paraphrase what the health practitioner or the patient says using *dice* and *dice que*.
- Describe and elicit descriptions of recommendations by health-care practitioners.

Cultural humility

Students will demonstrate an awareness of how to respond to patients with cultural humility when learning about the following Hispanic culturally based concepts or practices:

- The use of complementary and alternative medicines (CAM) among some individuals from the traditional sector of the Hispanic patient population.
- Cultural beliefs around child weight and *fatalismo.*
- The cultural beliefs that may shape the responses to pain for some traditional Hispanic patients.

A. Reflexive verbs

1. Reflexive pronouns

Reflexive verbs are easily recognized in Spanish because they have the reflexive pronoun *se* "oneself" attached to the infinitive form. (*Llamarse*), (*levantarse*) and (*ducharse*) are reflexive verbs.

2. Conjugating reflexive verbs

When a reflexive verb is conjugated or used in the infinitive form the reflexive pronoun must agree with the subject. *Yo = **me**, tú = **te**, él, ella, usted = **se**, nosotros = **nos**, ellos, ellas, ustedes = **se**.*

3. Vocabulary of verbs used during a physical examination

To conduct a "physical examination" or *chequeo / examen médico* both reflexive and non-reflexive verbs are used in Spanish.

Reflexive verbs:

Levantarse	To get up
Ponerse de pie	To stand up
Sentarse e>ie	To sit
Subirse a la mesa de examinación	To get on
Bajarse de la mesa	To get off
Acostarse o>ue en la mesa	To lie down
boca arriba o boca abajo	Face up/down
Quitarse o sacarse la ropa	To take off
Ponerse la bata o la ropa	To put on a robe or clothes
Subirse la manga de la blusa, camisa o camiseta	To roll up a sleeve
Tocarse una parte del cuerpo	To touch
No moverse	To not move

Non-reflexive verbs:

Abrir la boca, los ojos	To open
bien, más	Wide, more
Cerrar e>ie	To close
Contener la respiración	To hold one's breath
Respirar normalmente, profundamente	
Decir "ah" e>i,	To say

Doblar	To bend
Levantar / bajar	
Inclinar	
Extender e>ie	
Mirar a la derecha, a la izquierda, arriba, abajo	
No (mover)	
Poner los talones contra la pared.	To place ones heels against the wall
Sacar la lengua	To stick out one's tongue
Toser	To cough
Tragar	To swallow
Seguir la luz, mi dedo	To follow the light, my finger

4. Commands with favor de

In order to instruct a patient during an examination, use the *favor de + infinitivo*:

> *Voy a examinarle la garganta. Favor de abrir la boca.*
> *Voy a escucharle el corazón. Favor de respirar profundamente.*
> *Voy a tomarle la temperatura. Favor de abrir la boca o levantar el brazo*

More instructions:

Apretar (e>ie)	To apply pressure on body part
Tomar la presión, el pulso, el peso, la estatura	Blood pressure, pulse, weight and height
Pesar	To weigh
Medir (e>i)	To measure
Sacar una foto / una radiografía	To take a photo or X-ray

5. More symptoms with (tener) or (sufrir de)

Acidez en el estómago	Heartburn
Alergias a	
Calambres en	Cramps

Confusión	
El pulso irregular, tener taquicardia	
Entumecimiento en	Numbness
Espasmos en	
Falta de apetito	
Falta de aire	Shortness of breath
Faringitis estreptocócica	Strep
Fatiga	
Flujo vaginal	Discharge
Hemorroides	
Hormigueo en	Tingling
La visión borrosa o doble	Blurry or double vision
Los ganglios (linfáticos) inflamados	Swollen glands
Parte del cuerpo hinchado / a	Swollen body part
Problemas para tragar	Difficulty swallowing
Sangre en las heces	Blood in the stool
Sensibilidad a la luz o a los ruidos	Light or noise sensitivity
Sudores	Sweats

 ¡OJO!

Do not use the possessives with the parts of the body. Use the definite article: *Favor de abrir **los** ojos, señorita.*

If you are giving a command using the informal register, don't forget to change your reflexive pronoun from "*se*" to "*te*": *Favor de no mover**te**.*

 Audio I chequeo médico

 Cultura I (CAM therapies and products)

Some Hispanic patients may reject Western medicine in favor of complementary and alternative medicines (CAM). CAM therapies and products can include folk traditions, *curanderismo* and hot/cold remedies.

The *curandero* is a traditional healer who uses herbs and a holistic approach to address illness. *Curanderismo* is practiced throughout most of Latin America and in US Hispanic communities. *Curanderos* use healing methods based on prescribing herbal teas, baths or by performing *limpias* or cleanings. The herbs prescribed by the curandero to treat traditional diagnoses can potentially interfere with a prescribed medication or a course of treatment. Some traditional diagnoses are: *Ataque de nervios* (nervous attack), *bilis* (rage), *caída de la mollera* (fallen fontanel), *empacho* (indigestion), *fatiga* (fatigue or shortness of breath), *frío de la matriz* (frozen womb), *mal aire* (bad air), *mal de ojo* (evil eye), *mal puesto* (sorcery), *pasmo* (cold or frozen face) and *susto* (fright-induced soul loss). *Santeros* and *espiritistas* practice spiritualism through mediums to help heal patients because in some communities spirits outside the body are thought to cause illnesses such as mental disorders. These are cultural interpretations of illnesses and their remedies. Medical practices that strive to maintain a balance between "hot" and "cold" conditions and therapies are also a popular practice among many Hispanics. For example: cancer, colic, upper respiratory infections, indigestion and pneumonia are considered cold conditions while hypertension, a sore throat and *susto* are considered hot. In some cases, patients may carry an *amuleto* (good luck charm) to ward off evil (Chong, 2002). It is critical to address the patient's understanding of an illness before a course of treatment is put in place.

 ### *Práctica escrita I*

*Escribir la forma del infinitivo del verbo reflexivo o no reflexivo necesario en un examen médico para estos contextos. (**No conjugar el verbo** e incluir todas las posibilidades):*

1. Necesita mirar la garganta de su paciente.
2. Quiere confirmar que su paciente no tiene debilidad o mareos.
3. Su paciente artrítico tiene problemas con la rodilla. Quiere examinar la flexibilidad de las rodillas de su paciente.

4. Su paciente está sentado en una silla. Necesita mirar su abdomen en una posición horizontal.
5. Usted quiere verificar si su paciente tiene una neumonía.
6. Su paciente está en la mesa de examinación y necesita volver a su silla o asiento. (seat)
7. Quiere examinar la visión de su paciente que posiblemente tiene una concusión.

Práctica escrita 2

La ropa. Usted es enfermera. Crear instrucciones en español para sus pacientes antes del examen médico. Usar el vocabulario de la ropa, la expresión: "favor de" y los verbos: (ponerse) o (quitarse) / (sacarse) para estas situaciones:

1. The podiatrist wants to examine the right ankle of the patient who is wearing a skirt, tights and boots.
2. The gynecologist is going to do a pap-smear. The patient is wearing jeans and undergarments.
3. The doctor wants to conduct a breast examination and the patient is wearing a coat, a sweater and a bra.
4. The orthopedist is going to examine a male patient's lower back. He is wearing a t-shirt and a jacket.
5. The pediatrician is going to examine a boy's left toe. He is wearing socks and sneakers.
6. The urologist is going to examine a patient with prostate problems. He is wearing pants, a belt and sandals.
7. The technician is going to conduct an MRI for a young Mexican American female patient wearing leggings with a metallic zipper, a silver watch and silver earrings.
8. The generalist is checking a boy's head for a concussion. It is a cold day and he is wearing a wool cap.
9. The eye doctor is ready to conduct an eye examination and the patient is wearing contact lenses.

Práctica escrita 3

La ropa y los síntomas. It is winter and *enfermera* Ruiz gives instructions to a group of patients before each one heads off to see their doctor. What articles of clothing and/or accessories is she likely to instruct them to take off? Give all the possibilities:

1. La paciente tiene flujo vaginal.
2. El paciente tiene calambres en la pierna derecha.
3. Doña Luisa sufre de hemorroides.

4. El paciente sufre de entumecimiento en el brazo izquierdo.
5. El paciente de 84 años sufre de falta de aire.
6. La paciente tiene la visión borrosa.
7. El niño tiene el tobillo hinchado.

 ### Práctica escrita 4

Un chequeo médico. Put these commands in the correct chronological order:

1. (Favor de...) Bajarse de la mesa, tragar, levantarse, abrir la boca, ponerse de pie, subirse a la mesa, toser, cerrar la boca, decir "ah", sacar la lengua.
2. (Favor de...) Abrir los ojos, ponerse de pie, subirse a la mesa, sentarse, seguir la luz, levantarse, bajarse de la mesa.
3. (Favor de...) Acostarse boca arriba, bajarse de la mesa, levantarse, levantar el brazo, subirse a la mesa, doblar el brazo, ponerse de pie, extender el brazo.

 ### Práctica escrita 5

Chequeo médico. Give instructions appropriate to the task using *favor de + infinitivo*. The patient is sitting in a chair in the examination room. Make sure he gets on the table and then back to his seat.

1. The patient has an upper respiratory issue.
2. The patient thinks he fractured his knee.
3. The patient thinks he may have a concussion.

 ### Cultura 2 (obesity)

When discussing an infant's or a child's weight with parents during a medical encounter, the healthcare professional or staff should take into consideration that some Hispanics equate fatness with health in children (Kumanyika and Grier, 2006; Lindsay et al., 2011). Hispanic mothers and grandmothers, who often take on the role of caregiver and meal planner, are not likely to perceive their child as overweight (Hackie, 2007). Consequently, parents may be puzzled if a dietary suggestion is made by the health provider because they perceive their child to be healthy. In some families, parents may even regard a slender child to be malnourished and may employ pressure-to-eat feeding practices

(Martinez et al., 2017; Ochoa and Berge, 2017). In addition, there could be an expectation from the parent that the healthcare professional will also be concerned with the child's weight and will readily prescribe vitamins or dietary supplements. These cultural perceptions about children's weight along with feelings of *fatalismo* (the cultural belief in a predisposition to suffering chronic disease and to being obese) can affect healthy eating practices because parents may take minimal action to improve their health and that of their children. There is also some evidence that other home environment factors are associated with child obesity such as screen time, sedentary behavior and socioeconomic status (Ochoa and Berge, 2017). Some studies recommend a reframing of discussions on child obesity to better address this cultural framework by focusing more on unhealthy eating practices rather than the actual weight of the child (Contento et al., 2003; Crawford et al., 2004). Finally, it has been suggested that dietary quality can be compromised as families assimilate more into US "mainstream" culture. Higher levels of acculturation can have negative effects on breast feeding and feeding practices as well as on the quality of the diet consumed, especially from those coming to the US from rural areas (Pérez-Escamilla, 2009).

B. Pain management

I. Asking about pain

To ask questions about the location of pain or types of pain, use the verbs (*doler*), (*molestar*), (*tener*) or (*ser*) as indicated below. Please note that the stem-changer verb (*doler*) and regular verb (*molestar*) follow the same conjugation rules as the verb (*gustar*) and should always be preceded by the appropriate indirect object pronouns: *me, te, le, nos, les.*

> *¿Tiene dolor aquí? ¿Le duele aquí? ¿Le molesta aquí?*
> *¿Tiene dolor en el/la + parte del cuerpo? ¿Le duele el estómago? ¿Le molesta la rodilla?*
> *¿Tiene/Es un dolor leve (de 0 a 3), moderado (de 4 a 6), intenso (de 7 a 10)?*
> *¿Tiene/Es un dolor constante o intermitente?*

¿Tiene / Es un dolor punzante? (stabbing), *pulsante* (throbbing) *o ardiente?* (burning)

¿Tiene / Es un dolor profundo (deep) *o superficial?* (shallow)

¿Tiene / Es un dolor agudo (menos de 6 meses de duración) o crónico (más de 6 meses)?

¿Cuánto tiempo hace que le duele o que tiene este dolor? ¿Hace más de 24 horas, más de una semana?

¿Es mejor o peor el dolor cuando come? (¿descansa? ¿duerme? ¿camina? ¿corre? toma medicamento?)

2. Talking about medication

Generally the verbs (*tomar*) and (*usar*) are used in Spanish to talk about medication intake. (*Tomar*) is for medication taken orally, while (*usar*) is used for all other applications. Prescribed medication is *con receta*. Over the counter is *sin receta*.

Medicamentos o medicina y el verbo (tomar):

Un analgésico o comprimido para el dolor (un Tylenol)   a pain killer
Un antibiótico
Un antihistamínico
Un antiinflamatorio
Un antiácido
Un calmante
Un descongestionante
Un esteroide
Un expectorante
Un jarabe para la tos
Un laxante
Un sedante
Un supositorio
Vitaminas

If the medication is in liquid form, use:

en líquido o en jarabe. (dosage: *una cucharada, media cucharada, una cucharadita, una cucharadita y media, milímetros.*)

If it is a pill, use *en comprimido o cápsula*:

Generalmente tomo un antibiótico en comprimido. Pero mi hijo prefiere un antibiótico en líquido.

Medicamentos y medicina y el verbo (usar):

Gotas para los ojos	drops
insulina	
Un inhalador de albuterol	
Una crema (o pomada) para la piel.	
Un ungüento	ointment

 ¡OJO!

The verb (*molestar*) is a false cognate. It means to bother or give discomfort. *Me molestan las muñecas hoy* means: My wrists are bothering me today.

 Audio 2 los medicamentos

 Una conversación breve

—Buenos días, Juanito.

—Buenos días, doctor.

—¿Dónde tienes dolor?

—Me duele mucho la rodilla derecha, doctor. (*Many Mexican American speakers of Spanish use "rodilla" to mean the whole leg. Make sure you confirm if the patient is talking about his knee or leg.)

—Favor de subirte a la mesa de examinación y sentarte, por favor.

—Muy bien, doctor.

—Juanito, voy a tocarte la rodilla y apretar un poco. ¿Te duele aquí?

—Sí, me duele mucho.

—Favor de doblar la pierna, Juanito.

—No puedo, doctor. Me molesta mucho.

—¿Es un dolor intermitente o constante?

—Es constante. Me duele todo el tiempo, pero es peor cuando camino o doblo la pierna.

—¿Cuánto tiempo hace que tienes este dolor, Juanito?

—Hace dos semanas, más o menos.

—¿Te duele el tobillo también?

—No, doctor. Solamente me duele la rodilla en esta pierna.

—¿Tomas algo para el dolor?

—No, doctor. Necesito una receta para un analgésico por favor.

—¿Te gusta más en comprimido o en líquido?

—Un jarabe por favor. Tengo dificultad para tragar comprimidos.

—Muy bien. La enfermera Ruiz Delgado te va a sacar unas radiografías primero y después te escribo la receta.

—Gracias, doctor.

Cultura **3 (pain management)**

Responses to pain are subjective and can be culturally shaped by beliefs about addiction, religious coping, by socioeconomics and by dependence on CAM therapies. The majority of the national surveys conducted on the subject of pain have found that Hispanics report fewer pain conditions than non-Hispanic whites and non-Hispanic black respondents. There is some evidence that some Hispanics are more likely to report using religious coping in response to pain (Hollingshead et al., 2016). In some Hispanic traditional communities, *machismo* (a strong sense of masculinity) may frame a more stoic and gendered response to pain by sectors of the male population. However, pain varies with the individual and the level of acculturation. Learning from patients through conversations about pain expectations and perceptions can be useful to both practitioners and patients when prescribing medication. Providers should inquire about patients' use of cultural remedies or any off-label medications used for pain management in order to consider potentially dangerous drug interactions and educate patients about the risks in using illegally obtained drugs or medications (Hollingshead et al., 2016).

Source: www.eurekalert.org/pub_releases/2016-03/iuui-ipe031516.php

 Práctica escrita 6

Síntomas y medicamentos. Escribir una lista de medicinas y sugerencias (expresiones de obligación) para estos problemas.
   Modelo: High cholesterol: comer carne una vez por semana, hacer ejercicios aeróbicos 4 veces por semana, tomar comprimidos de Lipitor, perder peso.

1. A swollen knee:
2. Bronchitis:
3. A high fever:
4. An itchy rash:
5. A very high blood sugar reading:
6. An asthma attack:
7. A cold:
8. A debilitating back ache:

9. Conjunctivitis in one eye:
10. Insomnia:
11. Arthritis:

 Práctica escrita 7

Preguntas de comprensión. Create a fictitious identity and profile, and answer these questions.

1. ¿Con qué frecuencia tiene usted un examen médico?
2. ¿Quién es su médico de cabecera?
3. ¿Le duele una parte del cuerpo en este momento? ¿Qué parte? ¿Cuánto tiempo hace que tiene este dolor?
4. ¿Qué toma usted cuando tiene dolor de cabeza?
5. ¿Toma usted un jarabe cuando tiene tos?
6. ¿Tiene usted alergias? ¿Usa usted un inhalador?¿Quién más en su familia tiene alergias?
7. ¿Toma usted vitaminas cada día? ¿Necesita tomar vitamina D?
8. ¿Tiene usted problemas con los ojos? ¿Usa gotas?
9. ¿Es usted diabético? ¿Necesita inyecciones de insulina o toma usted comprimidos?
10. ¿Tiene usted mareos cuando se pone de pie rápidamente?
11. ¿Le molestan las rodillas cuando corre? ¿Qué tipo de dolor es?

C. What does the doctor say?

1. The verb (decir)

The verb (*decir*) means to "tell" or to "say." It should not be confused with the verbs (*hablar*) or (*conversar*) which mean to "talk" or to "converse."

2. Conjugating (tener) and (decir)

Like the verb (*tener*), (*decir*) is a stem changer, but it is an e>i and not an e>ie. Like all stem changers in the present tense, the infinitive form and the *nosotros* do not have a change. It is also irregular in the first person or *yo* form (-go).

Tener:	Decir:
Yo tengo	*Yo digo*
Tú tienes	*Tú dices*
Él, ella, usted tiene	*Él, ella, usted dice*
Nosotros tenemos	*Nosotros decimos*
Ellos, ellas, Uds, tienen	*Ellos, ellas, Uds dicen*

3. The expression decir que

The verb (*decir*) is frequently followed by the pronoun *que* to mean "that" when using indirect discourse to tell what someone is saying to someone.

*Él **dice** "buenos días". Él **dice que** necesita una cita.*

Audio 3 el verbo (decir)

Práctica escrita 8

Escribir <u>decir</u> o <u>decir que</u> según el contexto:

1. El paciente _____ "ah".
2. Nosotros _____ no nos gusta la carne.
3. Tú _____ tu nivel de azúcar es alto.
4. Yo _____ "hasta mañana" cuando salgo del salón de clases.
5. Los médicos _____ necesitas tomar un antibiótico durante una semana.
6. Usted _____ el endocrinólogo es su hermano.

Práctica escrita 9

¿Qué dice el médico? Write both what the doctor would say the patient do and not do under these circumstances:

Modelo: El paciente tiene fiebre. *El médico dice que el paciente debe (tiene que, necesita) tomar una aspirina cada 4 horas. El médico dice que el paciente no debe trabajar hoy.*

1. El paciente tiene una infección en el brazo.
2. El paciente tiene insomnio.
3. El paciente tiene conjuntivitis.
4. El paciente es anémico.
5. El paciente es obeso.
6. El paciente tiene intoxicación.
7. El paciente tiene picazón en la piel.
8. El paciente tiene ansiedad.
9. El paciente tiene diarrea y vómitos pero tiene mucha sed.

Audio 4 examen médico-práctico

El examen médico. Escuchar la conversación entre el médico y su paciente. Escribir el número de 1–14 para los tópicos de conversación que usted escucha, en orden cronológico. Write the number of the sequence of the topic you hear discussed (if the topic was not discussed at all, leave it blank):

_____ Farewells
_____ Symptoms of the patient
_____ Weather
_____ Type of pain
_____ Greetings
_____ Doctor recommendations
_____ Family
_____ Names
_____ Patient occupation
_____ Nationality of the patient
_____ Medicine patient is currently taking
_____ Medicine patient ought to be taking
_____ Duration of the pain
_____ Time
_____ Weight of patient

Audio 5

El chequeo médico: Escuchar la conversación entre el médico y su paciente. You will hear a conversation between a doctor and his 33-year-old patient. The doctor is giving the patient instructions in Spanish order to perform a medical exam. Circle the instructions that you hear:

Open your mouth.
Breathe deeply.
Stand up.
Get down from the table.
Look at the light.
Say ah.
Hold your breath.
Cough.
Extend your right arm.
Bend your knee.
Lie down on your stomach.
Stick out your tongue.
Get on the examination table.
Sit down.

Práctica escrita 10

Descripción y narración. Create a story around this picture using your imagination and creativity for what you can't see or don't know. First, describe the people in the image. (Occupations, physical aspects, age, names, clothing that they are wearing.) Then say what they do during the examination using the present tense. Be careful with stem changers like *acostarse* (o >ue), *sentarse* (e >ie), and *ponerse* (*cambio en el yo: -go*).

Use transition words to give a chronology: *Primero, luego, después, más tarde, al final.*

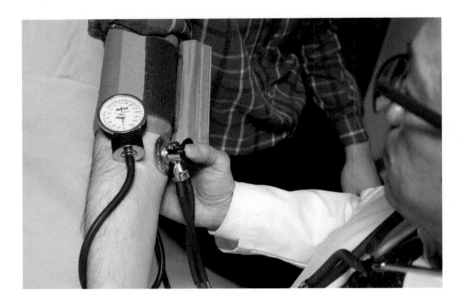

Práctica escrita 11

Descripción y narración. Create a story around this picture using your imagination. Don't be afraid to be creative. A) First describe the people in the picture and outside of the frame (location, physical aspects, personality traits, age, names, family members present, clothing that they are wearing, etc.) using 10 sentences and the verbs (*haber*), (*estar*), (*tener*) and (*llevar*). B) After your description, explain 4 things that the pediatrician does during the examination. Use the present tense of the verbs: (*saludar*), (*conversar*), (*decir*), (*levantar*), (*poner*), (*examinar*), (*mirar*), (*escuchar*), (*preguntar*) and (*contestar*), and use transition words to give a chronology to these actions (*primero, luego, después, más tarde, al final*).

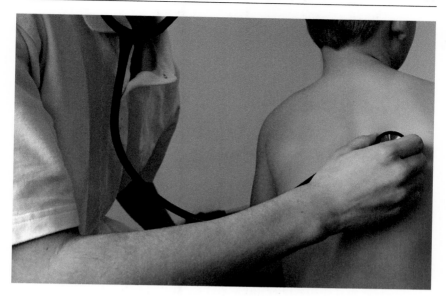

Role-play I

Voy a examinarle. You are a nurse and you meet with a new 20-year-old patient who complains of stomach pains:

Greet the patient.
Introduce yourself.
Find out her full name.
Ask her for her nationality.
Ask her for the name of her insurance and policy number.
Ask how she is feeling.
Ask her for her weight.
Tell her that you are going to examine her.
Give her instructions in chronological order to get her lying on her back.
Press down on the abdomen area and ask if it hurts (on the right, on the left, up and down).
Ask her what type of pain it is.
Ask her how long she has had that pain.
Ask her if it is better when she takes pain pills.
Suggest that she make an appointment with the internist.
Thank her.
Close.

(Vary the content of the simulation by providing different parts of the body in pain).

Role-play 2

Voy a examinarle. You are a pediatrician and you meet with a 7-year-old child with a swollen ankle and her mother:

Greet the patient and mother.
Make a comment about the beautiful sunny day.
Introduce yourself.
Ask the mother for her name and her daughter's name.
Compliment the child on her pretty dress.
Ask how she is feeling.
Tell her that you are going to examine her.
Give her instructions in chronological order to get her lying on the table.
Ask her to raise her ankle.
Press down and ask if it hurts.
Ask her how long she has had that pain.
Ask her if it is worse when she walks.
Suggest that she rest her ankle and not walk at all.
Thank them.

(Vary the content of the simulation by providing different parts of the body).

Role-play 3

Voy a examinarle. You are a family doctor and you meet with a 70-year-old man complaining of migraines. (After you become comfortable with the structure of this role-play, vary the complaints of the patient and the instructions of the medical examination to fit the ailment):

Greet your new patient.
Introduce yourself.
Exchange pleasantries about the weather.
Ask for his complete name and his age.
Ask him for physical symptoms.
He says his head hurts and he has a migraine.
Ask him how long he has had it.
Inform him that you are going to conduct a physical.
Get him on the examination table.
Ask if his neck hurts.
Touch parts of his head and ask if it hurts.
Ask if it hurts in another part of his body (*otra parte del cuerpo*).
Ask if he has difficulty talking or dizziness.
Ask him if he is congested or has a cold.

Ask him if he has allergies.
Ask him if he is stressed out or anxious.
Tell him that you are going to check his eyes.
Give instructions.
Comment that his eyes are bloodshot.
Ask him if his migraine is worse when he reads the paper (affirmative response).
Suggest that he make an appointment with an eye doctor.
Thank him for his visit.
Close.

 Práctica escrita 12

1. Write 2 role-plays that include an examination and questions about the nature of the pain. Incorporate old and new vocabulary when possible. In the first role-play, the patient is a 38-year-old housewife with asthma. In the second, the patient is a 43-year-old mechanic complaining of arm pain and palpitations.

Bibliography

Baughcum, Amy E. et al. "Maternal Feeding Practices and Childhood Obesity: A Focus Group Study of Low-Income Mothers." *Archives of Pediatrics & Adolescent Medicine*, vol. 152, 1998, 1010–1014.

Campbell, Claudia M. and Edwards, Robert R. "Ethnic Differences in Pain and Pain Management." *Pain Management,* vol. 2, no. 3, 2012, 219–230.

Christensen, Pia. "The Health-Promoting Family: A Conceptual Framework for Future Research." *Social Science & Medicine*, vol. 59, no. 2, 2004, 377–387.

Chong, Nilda. "Cultural Values of the Latino Patient," *The Latino Patient.* Intercultural Press, Boston, MA, 2002.

Contento, Isobel R. et al. "Body Image, Weight and Food Choices of Latina Women and Their Children." *Journal of Nutrition Education and Behavior*, vol. 35, no. 5, 2003, 236–248.

Crawford, Patricia B. et al. "Counseling Latina Mothers of Preschool Children about Weight Issues: Suggestions for a New Framework." *Journal of the American Dietetic Association*, vol. 104, 2004, 387–394.

Gropper, Rena C. *Culture and the Clinical Encounter: An Intercultural Sensitizer for the Health Professions.* Intercultural Press, Inc., Boston, MA, 1996.

Hackie, Mary. "Maternal Perception of Their Overweight Children." *Public Health Nursing*, vol. 24, no. 6, 2007, 538–546.

Hollingshead, Nicole A. et al. "The Pain Experience of Hispanic Americans: A Critical Literature Review and Conceptual Model." *The Journal of Pain: Official Journal of the American Pain Society*, vol. 17, no. 5, 2016, 513–528.

Juckett, Gregory. "Caring for Latino Patients." *American Family Physician*, vol. 87, no. 1, 2013, 48–54.

Kumanyika, Shiriki and Grier, Sonya. "Targeting Interventions for Ethnic Minority and Low-income Populations." *The Future of Children*, vol. 16, no. 1, 2006, 187–207.

Lindsay, Ana C. et al. "Latina Mothers' Beliefs and Practices Related to Weight Status, Feeding, and the Development of Child Overweight." *Public Health Nursing*, vol. 28, no. 2, 2011, 107–118.

Martinez, Suzanna M. et al. "Latino Mothers' Beliefs about Child Weight and Family Health." *Public Health Nutrition*, vol. 20, no. 6, 2017, 1099–1106.

Ochoa, Alejandra and Berge, Jerica M. "Home Environmental Influences on Childhood Obesity in the Latino Population: A Decade Review of Literature." *Journal of Immigrant and Minority Health*, vol. 19, no. 2, 2017, 430–447.

Pérez-Escamilla, Rafael. "Dietary Quality among Latinos: Is Acculturation Making Us Sick?" *Journal of the American Dietetic Association*, vol. 109, no. 6, 2009, 988–991.

Pulgarón, Elizabeth R. et al. "Hispanic Children and the Obesity Epidemic: Exploring the Role of Abuelas." *Families, Systems & Health: The Journal of Collaborative Family Healthcare*, vol. 31, no. 3, 2013, 274–279.

Reifsnider, Elizabeth et al. "Perceptions of Children's Body Sizes among Mothers Living on the Texas-Mexico Border (La Frontera)." *Public Health Nursing*, vol. 23, no. 6, 2006, 488–495.

Chapter 12

Taking past medical histories

LEARNING OUTCOMES FOR CHAPTER 12

Oral proficiency

Students will acquire the oral communicative skills that will allow them to appropriately interact in Spanish with their patients in the following ways:

- Describe and elicit descriptions about the past using the present perfect tense.
- Describe and elicit responses about past symptoms using the present perfect tense.
- Describe and elicit responses about medication intake and habits using the present perfect tense.
- Describe and elicit responses about whereabouts in the recent past using the present perfect tense.
- Take a medical history of a patient.

Cultural humility

Students will demonstrate an awareness of the practice of reporting pregnancies without including information on miscarriages and stillbirths, by some patients.

- They will demonstrate a culturally nuanced awareness about substance abuse and its relationship to gender, socioeconomic status and acculturation levels.

A. Talking about the recent past

I. The present perfect. Haber + ado / ido

The present perfect tense is used in Spanish to talk about the recent past and when taking a patient's medical history. It is called a "compound" tense because it is composed of 2 parts: a helping verb (*haber*) conjugated in the present tense, and a past participle that ends in ado/ido. The tense is formed like the compound verb in English ("have + ____-ed").

The present tense (a "simple" tense)	The present perfect tense (a "compound" tense)
Yo <u>uso</u>	Yo he <u>usado</u>
Yo <u>tomo</u>	Yo he <u>tomado</u>
Yo <u>tengo</u>	Yo he <u>tenido</u>
Yo <u>estoy</u>	Yo he <u>estado</u>

2. Morphology of (haber)

The verb (*haber*) in never conjugated in the present tense. It is invariable: *(no) hay*:

> **Hay** *un paciente enfermo en la sala de espera.*

However, in the present perfect tense, the verb is conjugated fully as the auxiliary or helping verb:

> *(Haber)*
>
> *Yo he*
> *Tú has*
> *El, ella, usted ha*
>
> *Nosotros hemos*
> *Ellos, ellas, ustedes han*

3. The regular past participle -ado / ido

The second part of the present perfect tense is called the past participle. In order to form the past participle for -*ar* verbs, drop the -*ar* of the infinitive and add: -*ado*.

Tomar	*tom-* + *ado*	= *tomado*

For -*er* and -*ir* verbs add -*ido*

Comer	*com-* + *ido*	= *comido*
Seguir	*segu-* + *ido*	= *seguido*

4. Irregular forms for the past participle

Some verbs have irregular past participle forms:

Decir = dicho
Hacer = hecho
Ver = visto
Poner = puesto
Romper = roto
Ir = ido
Escribir = escrito
Inscribirse (to join as in a gym) = inscrito

 ¡OJO!

In the present perfect the reflexive pronouns (*me, te, se, nos, se*) are always placed before the verb (*haber*).

Yo me <u>he levantado</u> a las ocho esta mañana.

 Audio I el pasado reciente

 Una conversación breve

—Buenas tardes, doctora Martínez Garau.
—Buenas tardes, Rosa. ¿Cómo estás hoy?
—Doctora, esta semana he sentido náuseas y he tenido frecuentes mareos.
—Rosa, ¿has comido bien esta semana?
—Sí, doctora. He desayunado, he almorzado y he cenado muy bien en casa todos los días.
—¿Cuántos vasos de agua has bebido hoy? ¿Estás deshidratada?
—No, he bebido 6 vasos de agua hoy.
—Bien, ¿has tenido dolores u otras molestias esta semana pasada?
—No, doctora.
—¿Cómo has dormido estos días?
—Doctora, me he acostado temprano y he dormido 8 horas por día.
—¿Has bebido alcohol o tomado drogas?
—No, doctora. Yo no tomo.
—¿Estás embarazada?
—No, ¡solamente tengo 15 años!
—¿Has tenido estos síntomas alguna vez?
—No, doctora. ¡Nunca he tenido estos mareos tan fuertes!
—Favor de subirte a la mesa de examinación, por favor.

Práctica escrita 1

Escribir estos síntomas y estas descripciones en el pasado.

1. Hoy tengo vómitos.
    Esta mañana, yo
2. Hoy tienes mucha fiebre.
    Esta semana, tú
3. En este momento usted tiene los ojos llorosos.
    Esta tarde, usted
4. Ahora, el paciente tiene ansiedad.
    El año pasado, el paciente
5. Ahora tenemos dolor de cabeza.
    El lunes pasado, nosotros
6. El niño es anémico.
    En el pasado, el niño
7. Ahora la madre del paciente es depresiva.
    La semana pasada, la madre del paciente
8. Ahora ustedes son delgados.
    En el pasado, ustedes (ser) besos.

Práctica escrita 2

*Doña Luisa, la nueva paciente de la doctora Pérez, contesta estas pre-
guntas sobre su historia médica y sus hábitos. Doña Luisa tiene 40 años.
Es diabética y tiene problemas de hipertensión. No lleva una vida saludable y no controla su dieta adecuadamente. Contestar las preguntas de la
médica:*
    Doña Luisa, recientemente...

1. ¿Ha tomado usted antibióticos?
2. ¿Ha fumado usted cigarrillos?
3. ¿Ha bebido usted más de dos vasos de agua cada día?
4. ¿Ha dormido usted menos de 6 horas por noche?
5. ¿Ha desayunado usted todos los días?
6. ¿Ha comido usted en restaurantes de comida rápida, en el trabajo o
    en casa?
7. ¿Ha consumido comida procesada más de dos veces por semana?
8. ¿Ha bebido alcohol todos los días? ¿Cuántos vasos o copas por día?
9. ¿Ha tomado usted sedantes?
10. ¿Ha tomado usted drogas?
11. ¿Ha ido a emergencias recientemente?
12. ¿Ha hecho ejercicios cardiovasculares? ¿Cuántas horas de ejercicios
    cardiovasculares o de otra actividad física ha hecho esta semana?

Práctica escrita 3

¿Dónde ha estado esta mañana? Where have you been? *Usted busca a su paciente de 50 años, don Lalo, que ha estado en el hospital con visitas a especialistas y exámenes de sangre. Finalmente por la tarde, él llega a su consultorio y usted le pregunta si (if) él ha estado en o ha ido a estos lugares esta mañana:*

Modelo: Has he been in the coffee shop? *¿Ha estado usted en el café del hospital esta mañana?*

Has he...
1. been in the waiting room on the fourth floor of the main building?
2. gone to the cafeteria?
3. shopped for a gift for his friend at the gift store?
4. been in the lab?
5. visited his cardiologist?
6. been close to nephrology?
7. gone to the intensive care unit?
8. talked to a doctor in emergency?
9. picked up medication at the pharmacy.
10. been in surgery.
11. gone over to the nurse's station to talk to his nurse?
12. visited a friend in the maternity ward.
13. completed forms at the administrative offices.

---

5. Time expressions for the recent past

Use these time expressions to talk about the recent past:

Esta mañana, esta tarde, esta noche
La semana pasada, el fin de semana pasado, el mes pasado, este año pasado
Este lunes pasado, este martes...
Recientemente, en el pasado
Antes de, después de (+ noun or + infinitive) *Antes de comer, antes de la clase*
Desde (since):
¿Ha tenido un problema con las rodillas desde la última visita?

Audio 2 expresiones de tiempo en el pasado

Práctica oral 1

With a colleague look at your planner and tell one another where you have been in the hospital this week and on what particular days.

<u>Modelo</u>: *Este lunes pasado he estado en el salón de clases en el edificio* _____, *en el estacionamiento de la calle* _____ *y en el departamento de* _____.

 Práctica escrita 4

Enfermero Sánchez habla con su paciente doña Ana. Ella siempre ha tenido problemas para controlar su obesidad y su dieta. Después de tres meses de ausencia, ella llega a su cita médica. Ahora, está muy delgada y le dice al enfermero que recientemente ha perdido mucho peso (20 libras). El enfermero le pregunta sobre su reciente pérdida de peso, su dieta y sus actividades físicas. Contestar las preguntas del enfermero:

Doña Luisa,
1. ¿Cuántas libras ha perdido usted?
2. ¿Se ha inscrito en un gimnasio recientemente?
3. ¿Qué tipo de actividad física ha hecho en los últimos meses?
4. ¿Cuántas veces por semana ha hecho estas actividades?
5. ¿Ha seguido una dieta nueva desde nuestra última conversación?
6. ¿Qué tipo de comidas ha eliminado de su dieta anterior?
7. ¿Ha comido con menos frecuencia en restaurantes de comida rápida?
8. ¿Quién ha preparado las comidas en casa?
9. ¿Ha eliminado su consumo de comida chatarra por la noche cuando mira la tele?
10. ¿Cómo han sido las porciones que se ha servido?
11. ¿Ha bebido más agua?
12. ¿Ha limitado el número de bebidas alcohólicas que consume cada día?
13. ¿Ha tenido mucha sed?
14. ¿En los últimos meses ha orinado excesivamente?
15. ¿Ha sufrido de fatiga?

 Práctica oral 2

Entrevista en parejas. Usted charla con su paciente de 52 años, doña Isabel. Su paciente dice que tiene poca energía, ha estado muy mareada estos días y se siente generalmente decaída:

1. ¿Ha ido al gimnasio esta mañana?
2. ¿Qué ha desayunado usted hoy? ¿Ha comido avena o huevos con tocino o salchichas?

3. ¿Cuántas ensaladas y cuántas porciones de vegetales ha comido usted esta semana?
4. ¿Ha comido sus espinacas regularmente?
5. ¿Ha tomado su medicina para controlar el colesterol?
6. ¿Ha tomado diariamente sus vitaminas?
7. ¿Cuántas horas ha dormido por la noche estos últimos días?
8. ¿Cuántos vasos de agua ha bebido hoy?
9. ¿Ha tenido estrés en el trabajo o con su familia?
10. ¿Ha hecho meditación?
11. ¿Ha dejado de fumar?
12. ¿Ha limitado su consumo de alcohol?
13. ¿Cómo ha tenido la tensión, alta o baja?
14. ¿Ha sufrido de palpitaciones?
15. ¿Ha sufrido de falta de aire?

 Práctica oral 3

Circular en la clase y preguntar a sus colegas sobre esta semana pasada. ¿A qué lugares han ido?, ¿qué días? y ¿para hacer qué actividad?

   <u>Modelo</u>: *El hospital: Sí, he ido al hospital para consultar con un colega, este sábado pasado.*

Lugar	Para qué	Cuándo	Nombre del estudiante
I. La gasolinera	I.	I.	I.
2. El mercado biológico	2.	2.	2.
3. Un café	3.	3.	3.
4. La iglesia	4.	4.	4.
5. La oficina de correos	5.	5.	5.
6. Una librería	6.	6.	6.
7. Un restaurante mexicano	7.	7.	7.
8. Un restaurante italiano	8.	8.	8.
9. El banco	9.	9.	9.
10. La tintorería	10.	10.	10.

Después de terminar la actividad, reportar a la clase.

Práctica escrita 5

Formulario de historia médica del paciente. Completar el formulario con información personal y un perfil médico ficticio de una paciente de 63 años.

HISTORIA MÉDICA DEL PACIENTE

APELLIDO(S): _____

NOMBRE:_____

DIRECCIÓN:_____

NÚMERO DE TELÉFONO:_____

FECHA DE NACIMIENTO:_____

NOMBRE DEL SEGURO MEDICO:_____

NÚMERO DE PÓLIZA: _____

PREGUNTAS:

1. ¿Bebe o ha bebido alguna vez alcohol? ¿Cuánto bebe al día?
2. ¿Fuma o ha fumado alguna vez? ¿Cuántas cajetillas fuma por día / semana? ¿Cuándo ha dejado de fumar?
3. ¿Toma o ha tomado drogas alguna vez? ¿Cuándo? ¿Qué drogas?
4. ¿Toma algún medicamento ahora? ¿Cuáles?
5. ¿Ha tenido alguna vez una operación? ¿Cuántas y cuándo? ¿De qué tipo?
6. ¿Ha estado hospitalizado alguna vez en su vida? ¿Cuántas veces?
7. ¿Ha tenido palpitaciones recientemente?
8. ¿Ha tenido dificultad respiratoria recientemente?
9. ¿Ha tenido mareos recientemente?
10. ¿Ha estado usted embarazada? ¿Cuántas veces? ¿Ha tenido una pérdida fetal o un aborto natural?
11. ¿Tiene o ha tenido la tensión alta? ¿Baja?
12. ¿Ha tenido problemas digestivos? ¿Otros problemas serios?
13. ¿Cuándo ha tenido su último chequeo médico?
14. ¿Ha habido una historia en su familia de cáncer?
15. ¿Ha habido en su familia una historia de alergias?
16. ¿Ha habido en su familia una historia de hipertensión?
17. ¿Ha habido en su familia una historia de diabetes?
18. ¿Ha habido en su familia una historia de enfermedad cardíaca? ¿Otras enfermedades?

Cultura I (reporting pregnancies)

When taking a medical history and asking about past pregnancies, it is important for the nurse or health provider to specifically ask about miscarriages (*abortos naturales o abortos*) and stillbirths (*pérdidas fetales*). Some Hispanic women from rural areas may only mention past pregnancies that resulted in live births (Gropper, 1999).

Práctica oral 4

Historia médica de su paciente. Volver a la *Práctica escrita* 5 y usar el formulario para obtener la historia médica de su paciente. *Después, reportar la información recogida a la clase.*

Cultura 2 (substance abuse and alcoholism)

Hispanic adolescents have a higher risk than their White non-Hispanic and African American peers to develop a tendency toward substance abuse (Johnston, 2012). There is some evidence that Hispanic adolescents who assimilate into the US "mainstream culture" and lose their connection with their Hispanic culture are at a greater risk than those who maintain strong family and cultural protective ties (Szapocznik et al., 2007). While Hispanic adolescents may vary in their relationship with their culture of origin, their family and US "mainstream culture," it is important to understand how these cultural ties and varying perceptions of discrimination in the US can shape their dependence to substance abuse (Unger, 2014). Among Hispanic adults, men generally drink more than women and do so more heavily after migrating to the US (Chong, 2002). While Hispanic women are generally more likely to abstain from drinking than males, a number of investigations propose that those who hold US "mainstream cultural" values are more likely to drink heavily and become dependent on alcohol (Alvarez, 2007; Caetano et al., 2004). Similarly, Hispanic men at higher levels of acculturation to the US tend to drink more, but this effect is moderated by income. Men with above-average income are more likely to be drinkers (Karriker-Jaffe, 2009). Research also indicates that Puerto Ricans and Mexican Americans may be at higher risk of substance abuse than other Hispanics (Lee, 1997).

Role-play I

You are a doctor and meet with a new older patient who complains of sharp abdominal pains. (Vary the simulation by changing the complaint.)

Greet the patient.
Introduce yourself.
Exchange a pleasantry.
Ask the patient 5 questions in the present tense. Use (*ser, estar, tener, comer*) appropriately to get information about:

- Date of birth,
- Weight and height,
- Current general condition,
- Current symptoms,
- And general nutritional practices.

Ask the patient 5 past history questions using the present perfect tense around the following topics:

- Alcohol/drug consumption,
- Medication in-take,
- Hospitalizations,
- Family history, and
- Symptoms in the recent past

Make a recommendation.
Thank the patient for his visit.
Close the conversation.

Role-play 2

You are a nurse practitioner and you meet with a mother and her daughter (a 10-year-old) who has a significant rash on her back and legs. (Vary the simulation by changing the complaint.)

Greet mother and child.
Introduce yourself.
Ask the child for her first name.
Compliment the patient's dress.
Ask patient for her age, birthday and favorite food.
Ask the mother questions about the patient's current state:

- Current allergies to food or to medications,
- Frequency of rashes,
- Does she currently have a fever?

Ask the mother questions about the patient's medical history:

- What medications has she taken recently?
- Has she vomited today?
- Has she had a fever this week?
- Has she eaten something new recently?
- Has she used a new soap (*jabón*)?
- Has she worn new clothes? new undergarments?

Make a recommendation.
Close the conversation.

Bibliography

Alvarez, Josefina et al. "Substance Abuse Prevalence and Treatment among Latinos and Latinas." *Journal of Ethnicity in Substance Abuse*, vol. 6, no. 2, 2007, 115–141.

Caetano, Raul et al. "Acculturation, Drinking, and Intimate Partner Violence among Hispanic Couples in the United States: A Longitudinal Study." *Hispanic Journal of Behavioral Sciences*, vol. 26, 2004, 60–78.

Chong, Nilda. "Communicating Effectively with the Latino Patient," *The Latino Patient*. Intercultural Press, 2002, pp. 67–77.

Duggan, Catherine et al. "Diabetes Prevention in Hispanics: Report from a Randomized Controlled Trial." *Preventing Chronic Disease*, vol. 11, no. 28, 2014, 1–11.

Gropper, Rena C. *Culture and the Clinical Encounter. An Intercultural Sensitizer for the Health Professions*. Intercultural Press, Inc. 1996.

Johnston, Lloyd D. et al. "Monitoring the Future National Survey Results on Drug Use, 1975–2010: Volume I, Secondary School Students." Ann Arbor: Institute for Social Research, The University of Michigan, 2012.

Karriker-Jaffe, Katherine J. and Sarah E. Zemore. "Associations between Acculturation and Alcohol Consumption of Latino Men in the United States." *Journal of Studies on Alcohol and Drugs*, vol. 70, no. 1, 2009, 27–31.

Lee, DJ. "Epidemiology of Self-Reported Heavy Drinking in Hispanic Adults." *Ethnicity and Health*, vol. 2, 1997, 77–89.

Szapocznik, Jose et al. "Drug Abuse in African American and Hispanic Adolescents: Culture, Development, and Behavior." *Annual Review of Clinical Psychology*, vol. 3, 2007, 77–105.

Telzer, Eva H. et al. "Family Obligation Values and Family Assistance Behaviors: Protective and Risk Factors for Mexican-American Adolescents' Substance Use." *Journal of Youth and Adolescence*, vol. 43, no. 2, 2014, 270–283.

Unger, Jennifer B. "Cultural Influences on Substance Use among Hispanic Adolescents and Young Adults: Findings from Project RED." *Child Development Perspectives*, vol. 8, no. 1, 2014, 48–53.

Index

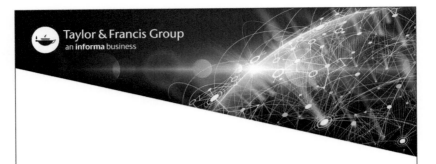